# CHAPTER ONE   INTRODUCTION

## 1.1  This Book's Purpose and Ambition

Here we go! This book describes a **new simple graphic device** that I have invented and I call **Employment Plots**. They are designed to help career analysis and planning and to show how **career progression** can be related to **occupations** within a comprehensive directory of **organisations.**   The aim is to clear the fog and bring employment situations into focus.

Serious stuff - and I take it seriously (though you may have the odd doubt as we go forward) - but I also intend the book to be entertaining, even humorous. Enjoyable **and** enlightening!

As far as I am aware the device is original, though I am pretty sure that some pedantic academics will come out of the woodwork to claim themselves progenitor, probably in some obscure publication like "Journal of Papers Submitted by University Academics to Gain Points for their Department". As they say, great minds think alike.

Even if Employment Plots are not original, I am almost certain that nobody has presented them in the style and substance you are about to enjoy. They are **artificial** constructs but, much like "*i*" (the square root of minus one), just because it does not exist does not mean that we cannot make use of it.

A simile is you observing fleas copulating under a microscope. I cannot help you directly to improve your chances in the flea mating game, but I can give you the tool (a microscope) to assist you in studying the reproductive cycle of fleas and therefore, indir through the provision of the microscope, improve your knowledge of their dirty habits.

The difference is that there is nothing dirty about your career or your occupation (maybe a little grime in your organisation). Despite the wry language and content of this book, its ambitions are particularly **serious**.

## 1.2 The Peter Principle

The initial idea for this book came from two inputs; the first was a re-reading of "The Peter Principle" by Dr. Lawrence J. Peter and Raymond C. Hull. *("The Peter Principle" published in paperback by the Souvenir Press, 2019 reprint, the publication that you are more likely to find at the airport than in your National Library.)*

The Peter Principle is:

*"In a Hierarchy every Employee Tends to Rise to*

*His level of Incompetence"*

This principle was announced to the world in the "international best seller" published a little over 50 years ago (intellectual property and copyright lawyers please note). Whilst it is not necessary to have read the book, for my purposes it is only required that you understand the principle, which is obvious only when you see it! Indeed, I have invested the sum of an overdue fine so that I could read my library copy twice for your benefit.

This re-reading began to stir some heretical puzzles:

(1) How come nobody thinks that the Principle applies to them?
(2) We all know at least someone who is incompetent and yet continues to be promoted.

# EMPLOYMENT PLOTS

A humorous introduction to a simple and novel graphic device which aids the analysis and planning of careers and occupations in a comprehensive range of organisations.

## Robin Linklater

All the rave reviews of this book have been removed at the request of the author, citing modesty. Perhaps it is because he has not yet worked out how to break into the professional puffers' magic circle.

## Dedication

To my Family (In lieu of money)

## Acknowledgements

My heartfelt thanks to Margaret, Beth, Fay, Richard and Stef for their input and proof reading. It is only fair that readers should know whom to blame for any errors: mea culpa.

## About the Author

Robin Linklater occupied his first twelve years under the employment yoke as an academic, ending up as a Senior Lecturer in Design Management at the then Leicester Polytechnic. He then vainly tried to turn theory into practice for the next fifteen years in UK retail at middle and senior levels. He retired early to lick his wounds.

He now spends the bulk of his time sulking.

# Contents

(3) We all know someone (fewer) who survive their careers without a blemish.

At first, I assumed that these doubts were a result of my limited intelligence but asking around my brighter associates provided no insights.

Dare I question the Everest of organisation theory? You will see that I do.

## 1.3  The Second Instigator

The second idea for this book came, perhaps surprisingly, from an article I was reading (for the first and last time) in a trusty Reader's Digest entitled "Everything You Need to Know about Physics" (condensed).

Apparently, in 1905 Albert Einstein published papers now referred to as his Special Theory of Relativity. He was delighted with his efforts because nobody but nobody understood a blind word.

Over the next decade, however, problems began to emerge. More and more people started to claim that they understood this Special Theory. Dear old Albert was increasingly concerned. What was the point of being the most famous scientist in the world if lots of others, in and out of his discipline, thought that his work was intelligible? To say that he was not best pleased was an understatement comparable to a galaxy. "My God," he was heard to cry, "What is the world coming to? Hold on a minute, that is a very interesting question which I must solve after tea." His personal hygiene began to suffer, he stopped going to the barbers and began to forget to trim his moustache.

The situation came to a head when, at a conference in Switzerland (at that young age he liked skiing) several university professors complained that their students were now dismissive, ("Yeah, yeah, yeah, Special Theory of Relativity. Been there, done that, move on.")

His answer came a decade later in his General Theory of Relativity, which included the famous equation ($E=MxCxC$) designed so that its scale was so big that nobody (including himself) could get their head around it

If you took C (the speed of light that equals 299,792,458 metres per second (roughly) and multiplied it by itself and then multiplied that by the mass of a house brick you got to a number so incredibly large that it was incomprehensible to anyone. Job done.

Mr. Einstein had, perhaps by accident, stumbled into a technique that was to become a standard of twentieth century science: sow confusion by generalising everything that could be tested, replacing experiment with theory.

## 1.4   Special and General Theories

The Peter Principle can only be applied to **hierarchical organisations.** The question that these two works inspired was this: was it possible to firstly question the Peter Principle (admittedly a foolhardy exercise) and secondly to take such an investigation into hierarchical organisations and broaden it to consider **non-hierarchical structures** of which, it turns out, there are quite a lot.

I aim to reverse Mr. Einstein's technique: the Peter Principle is assumed here to be a **Special Theory of Organisations** and this book outlines a corresponding **General Theory,** which firstly investigates what happens to employees after they reach their level of incompetence and secondly explores competence and incompetence in organisations that are not hierarchical.

Through perusal of this book you will be able to understand **all** organisations and not just those hierarchical ones covered in the Special Theory. You will understand much better your place in any organisation (and those of your colleagues) and be better able to plan your future career.

That therefore is the mission: **to study all work organisations, their occupations and people's careers within them and their interplay. The correspondence of organisations and careers for the purposes here is defined as "employment".**

The line:

"I am a Pigmy Standing on the Shoulders of Giants" is attributed to Bernard of Chartres and is popularly ascribed by Newton. I am the pigmy comfortably ensconced.

## 1.5  The Principle and the Book

One confusion that we must clear up to begin with is that between the Peter Principle itself and the annoyingly eponymous book. In my book here, I shall refer to the principle itself as "The Peter Principle" and the book as "Dr. Peter's work".

Obviously calling Dr. Peter's book throughout my book "Dr. Lawrence Peter's and Raymond C. Hull's book" would grow wearisome so I have taken the decision to excise Raymond Hull from further mention, but you should be assured full credit is given here for his contribution. Indeed some would argue that it really should be called "Raymond C. Hull's book" since, as he tells us in its introduction, he in fact wrote the masterpiece from notes and conversations with Dr. Peter himself.

Another reason for the excision is, how can I put this, Hull (now demoted from Raymond C. Hull) did not have a Ph.D., so is definitely a lesser light. You will have noticed that I also do not have a doctorate so it is not polite to cast aspersions. The excuse is the certainty of copious Honorary Doctorates that will accrue to this author very soon after this first edition, which will also allow him to update this volume for its second and subsequent editions.

Unlike Dr. Peter I do not have a Raymond Hull. Unlike Don Quixote I do not have a Sancho Panza; unlike Johnson I do not have a Boswell and, in due course I, no doubt, will not have a Vasari to my Leonardo. All my own work.

You will have noticed that Dr. Peter and Raymond C. Hull do not consider females in stating their principle (after all, it was fifty years ago) and I am not responsible for that but, please be reassured, all of my writing does, in fact, include women, and benefits thereby.

## 1.6  Book Structure

The theme of this book is that when two or more people meet in a common enterprise they form an **Organisation**; and their roles in that Organisation are determined by a concept called **Status**. Dr. Peter's work (The Special Theory) applies to hierarchical organisations with distinct levels. This **General Theory** shows that **all** organisations can be analysed in terms of career progress against occupation development.

So what is this General Theory about? After this introduction we describe the building, stage by stage, of **Employment Plots**, the fundamental simple visual pictograms which are the tools for plotting careers with occupations provided by organisations. Within this part, Chapter 2 introduces to the reader the concept of **Status,** which is the key determinant to be measured against time in both **Career Paths** (Chapter 3) and **Organisation Tracks,** which can be compared with each other in **Employment Plots** which make up Chapter 4.

Chapters 5 through 9 then demonstrate how we can use this new technique of Employment Plots to describe the full range of organisations likely to occur in working life. The bulk of analysis is given over to what I designate **Regular Organisations** (Chapters 5, 6 and 7.) Chapter 8 examines some **Time Aspects** and Chapter 9 looks at several types of **Irregular Organisations.**

Chapter 10 goes back to the Peter Principle and discovers that its comparison to Employment Plots realises important real-life facts (General Theory scrutinises the Special Theory as per Albert). Chapter 11 shows some further examples of the **practical application** of Employment Plots by exploring everyday career analysis and planning.

## 1.7 Book Style

Wikipedia (All Hail!) suggests that "Peters and Hull intended the book to be a satire but as it became popular it seemed to make a serious point about the shortcomings of how people are promoted within hierarchical organisations."

I am not ashamed to copy their style. This book is not an academic treatise arguing about how many angels can fit on a pinhead. It is deliberately **conversational and light-hearted** whilst, at the same time, it hopes to make serious points about life's ambitions, especially in the workplace. Usually there is nothing comical about organisation theory if you have to study it so, hopefully, this will be a modest respite. After all, many comic masterpieces deal with real and important human issues (e.g. Cosi, Catch 22, Rosenkavalier, King Lear!?) so why should not I try? The lightness of style should not blind you to my intentions: I have designed Employment Plots as a real and functional tool to lie contentedly in the annals of organisation theory.

To achieve this approach I have used **Case Studies** throughout. Again, these are not the sort of weighty and impenetrable case studies which students in Management Schools often grapple with. Here some are sober, some frivolous, all are expressly chosen to provoke attention and relate to ordinary life. Most importantly, they are short. Each Case Study is followed by a **Commentary** to drag you back to the thread. The idea is that the Case Studies will be easily memorable and the Commentaries will not only remind us of the relevance to Employment Plots but also try to relate their content to "Real life." Here is an example:

Case Study:  Publishing Nightmare

A Senior Lecturer in Hierarchy Studies (it is not I) gives up teaching (nobody notices) to write a major opus on something or other. She chooses a prospective publisher through extensive research (i.e. she Googled "How to get a book published") and sends off her opus with high hopes.

She does not hear anything for some time, so she begins to call the publisher to try to get things moving. She is passed "from pillar to post"; no one seems to have heard of her opus but all promise to seek it out from within the company. To no avail.

She complains of her dilemma in the Senior Common Room to an Early Adopter of a book called "Employment Plots". He recommends the author purchase a copy of this magnificent tome. She soon recognizes that the publisher organization is of the form "Regular Inclined" (Please wait until Chapter 5) so she changes tack.

She calls the publisher's receptionist and suggests that she would like to take someone on the staff to lunch. Immediately she is in touch with several members of staff who claim the authority to select her work for publication.

She selects the most likely candidate mainly on the basis that he has an MBA from the London School of Economics. He is a Senior Assistant Deputy Editor, and she takes him to lunch at a restaurant carefully selected to balance pecuniary with business considerations.

Their conversation seems to roam over many topics which appear, to the Senior Lecturer, to have nothing to do with her opus. At many points she actually doubts that the publisher has read the work in question.

After the hors d'oeuvres, but just before the second bottle of wine is opened, she asks the Senior Assistant Deputy Editor if he has a view on the opus. "Oh no", he replies, "I couldn't even find it, but that doesn't matter, really. Send me another copy."

Nothing has been mentioned concerning royalties which, to be frank, is the Senior Lecture's main interest (after fame amongst her academic circle), so she raises the issue.

The Senior Assistant Deputy Editor looks shocked. He says, "What we do is publish a first edition of, say, ten copies. If that sells out within a year we publish a second edition of one hundred thousand copies. Only when those sell out will we publish a third edition on which we pay you a royalty of a penny a copy."

The Senior Lecturer puts the lunch investment down to experience and self-publishes on Amazon. Fame if not fortune.

Commentary I guess that you would employ a dentist to fix your teeth and a solicitor to arrange your divorce. I heartily recommend that you employ experts in your life, not just dentists to fix your teeth or lawyers to manage your divorce but also in your business. The secret is to properly brief them on your problem, otherwise they will tend to hijack your project and turn it into one that can only be solved by their area of expertise. You have made an excellent start by buying this book written by this authority.

So why have I dissed publishers in this Case Study? It is to illustrate the importance of choosing the right expert; the Senior Lecturer should have approached a **literary agent** (who are all brilliant) as they are the experts in getting her opus in front of publishers without the need for entertaining (I think) and thus to market. Hopefully, at least one **literary agent** has got this far and I have got their attention and they realise that I think that they are **all wonderful**. And so are publishers, really.

## 1.8 Nomenclature

I am nearly British: born to an Irish mother and a Scottish father. Regretfully, have no English blood and cannot therefore be classed as truly British (so near and yet so far!)

Be that as it may, I have lived and worked in Great Britain all my life and regard myself as sort of ersatz British. I write here with British vocabulary. If I even tried to translate into American English I would be bound to get it wrong and offend my cousins from over the pond.

Thus it is "estate agent" and not "realtor", or "petrol" and not "gas". Actually I have no need to use these two words but I hope that the examples will suffice.

To make it a little easier, Capitalist readers can just multiply everything by ten. Oligarchs can go straight to the Case Study "Top of the Pile" in Chapter 2 and Communist readers can go straight to the Case Study "The Collective" in Chapter 9; easy to find as it's the only bit that isn't redacted in your country.

Throughout the book I have employed a technique to save me from the attention of pedants. I use many words that, for convenience, do not stand up to doctrinaire inspection. For example, you will be introduced to my concept of **Skills** which will be recognised as meaning skills in a roundabout way. I have distinguished such word approximations by capitalising them thus: "**S**kills", leaving the proper word "**s**kills" to its dictionary definitions.

"When I use a word," Humpty Dumpty said in a rather scornful tone, "it means just what I choose it to mean – neither more nor less."

"The question is, "said Alice, "whether you can make words mean so many different things."

"The question is, "said Humpty Dumpty, "which is to be master – that's all."

(*Lewis Carroll's "Through the Looking Glass"*)

## 1.9  Conclusions and Chapter's Key Points

In this Introduction I hope to have set you on your way with a bounce in your mental step. Please read on ...

**This book describes a new visual aid to organisation theory called Employment Plots**

**Its aim is to expand the Peter Principle to cover all organisations, not just hierarchical ones**

**This book's light-hearted style should not be confused with a lack of seriousness; it is meant to be enjoyable as well as instructive**

**It is in three parts:**

**The construction of Employment Plots**
**The application of Employment Plots to describe all organisations and aspects of time**
**Using Employment Plots for Career Analysis and Planning**

# CHAPTER 2  STATUS

## 2.1  Introduction to Status

Firstly, I recommend that you do not skip this chapter. It describes the key concept in the General Theory. If you happen to be reading this as a bedtime story to a child and they, perchance, fall asleep, then wake them up (repeatedly if necessary) and continue through the chapter. I am sure that, in the end, they will appreciate it. An exam will need to be passed before you are allowed to begin Chapter 3. This is a long Chapter; I cannot say, in all honesty, that you will have broken the back of my manuscript once through this, but perhaps it will give you hope.

The next three chapters describe the elements that go into making up Employment Plots:

Chapter 2 = The concept of Status

Chapter 3 = Pictograms displaying Status against time and Career Paths

Chapter 4 = Addition of Occupation Tracks to complete Employment Plots

My first proposition in developing Employment Plots is that when two or more people interact they establish a **hierarchy,** where places in that ranking are dependent on **Status** (Note the capital "S"). This is the first of my speculative assertions (there are more to come) for which I offer no academic or any other support.

This, and further notional designations in this book, make sense to me and I hope that they will for you too. If I were willing (and perhaps, able) to academically source and justify all I have to say then we would have a thesis in which the practicality and application of **Employment Plots** (which are the central idea in this book) would be drowned out. And this book would be a lot more expensive.

The proof of the pudding is in the eating; Employment Plots are intended as a means of looking at the Careers and Occupations in the workplace from an imaginative angle and not as rigorous argument.

Since **Status is the fundamental measure** that I use in my Employment Plots, I shall devote this whole Chapter to defining what I mean by it. Status as part of Employment Plots is a bit like weight as a part of the equation in Body Mass Indices: something needs to be compared with something else for it to mean anything.

As I have said, fundamental to Status is that when two or more people interact they **always** establish a hierarchy. This can be overt or covert, conscious or unconscious.

Examples:

Who became the servant and who became the master when Robinson Crusoe met Man Friday?

When a group meet at a restaurant for dinner, who sits at the head of the table? If that is not the person who is paying for the meal it could end up in arguments.

Two car drivers conduct a dialogue following a minor accident. Who shouts loudest? Where does the witness who tries to get involved stand?

Who is the most supercilious at the bridge table?

The suspect who says "No comment" to all questions at that "Interview under Caution" or his interrogator. Who has the upper hand?

Who is teacher's pet?

Who hogs the TV remote?

When several people meet, there will be a very complicated web of inter-related comparisons. This is called "ascertaining the pecking order". If people know each other well then only acknowledgements of minor changes in rankings are required. In large gatherings most of the content of the meeting is given over to fixing those rankings through discussing the agenda whilst supposedly talking to it.

I am assuming here that you want to **come out on top** in hierarchical situations and can achieve this by increasing your Status. As we will see, there are many organisations that are not hierarchical but the desire to augment Status is pretty universal.

## 2.2  Defining Status Part 1

The word "status" has a very broad meaning. I need to be more specific in what it means for this book; again my definition is designed for the purposes of constructing Employment Plots (I bet you cannot wait!) but I do think that it is relevant to real life.

Firstly, I want to break Total Status into two parts: **Work Status** and **Life Status** (please note the capitalisation of Work and Life). Work Status is that part of a person's Total Status derived from their occupation and Life Status is that derived from all other aspects of their existence.

As we go through life (note not capitalised, therefore as you normally understand the word) Life Status will make up the major part of Total

Status in childhood and after retirement from employment, whilst Work Status will (usually but not necessarily, it depends on the job) be dominant during your career. Hopefully, some Case Studies will help:

Case Studies: (a), (b) and (c) Scenes from Life

(a) A panhandler, complete with regulation dog (hungry looking, definitely not pedigree), shakes his paper cup at a passerby.

(b) A Human Resources Manager has a hectic and emotional day making twelve employees redundant. On her way home she calls into a bar and orders, from the barman, a large stiff drink.

(c) A child goes to bed, anxiously awaiting the arrival of the Tooth Fairy after losing a baby molar.

Commentary (a) panhandler is not in the slightest interested in the passerby's employment; his sole concern is his potential generosity. Possible Life Status of the passerby is more important than his Work Status.

(b) The Human Resources Manager is not in the least concerned with the barman's life outside of the bar; she just wants him to do his job and serve her a drink, any drink. The Work Status of the barman is paramount.

(c) The child (since she has been good about the dental loss) wakes in the morning to find that her parents' promises were well founded and the magic sprite has done her job. Life Status and Work Status are in balanced and in parallel.

We will continue with our research concentrating on the two discrete elements of Status. In the end, they will be combined for any person varying according to their individual circumstances.

This leads us to our next premise:

Life Status + Work Status = Total Status

With any luck you are still with me and some, examples will guide us:

Examples of Good and Bad Life and Work Statuse

Life Status (High/Low): Low Golf Handicap/Butter Fingers, Flawless Skin/Acne, Oratory/Mumbling, Master of Wine*/ Wino

Work Status (High/Low): Aircraft Pilot/White Van Man, A Beatle/ An Osmond, Three Star Chef/ Washer Upper, Politician/Politician, Wizard/Witch

* Master of Wine cannot be seen as Work since the holder of this honour will never, in his or her career, recoup the expenditure needed to achieve the qualification, however enjoyable the educational experience.

We are naturally concerned in this book with individual people but all sorts of things can have Status: dogs, football teams, governments. Anything, really.

## 2.3  Defining Status Part 2

In the General Theory the next hypothesis is that both Life and Work Statuses can be broken down into aspects of **Skills, Wealth** and **Esteem** (Again, please note the capitalisation, my definitions to follow.) You and I could think up other characterisations of granular status but this breakdown is for Status, not status, so please indulge me on this. For any individual these attributes can be represented in the form of bar charts should you wish to do so:

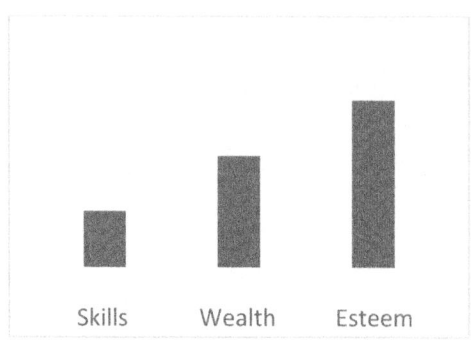

LIFE STATUS PROFILE

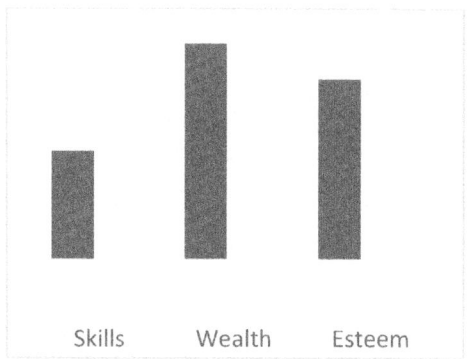

WORK STATUS PROFILE

These two Status Profiles pictograms are illustrative only and they are not scaled; they, and similar pictograms in this book, are designed to give ideas of quantities and the relationships between the elements.

Naturally, everyone will have different profiles for both Life and Work with diverse amounts of Skills, Wealth and Esteem. I am only guessing but I suspect that in your opinion your Work Status (exceptionally high Skills) beats your boss's (higher Wealth and Esteem but lousy Skills.)

The elements of Skills, Wealth and Esteem can be negative as well as positive: my skills at DIY certainly are and I am currently in debt. It is only my exceptional Esteem that keeps me up there.

Wealth and Esteem (in the terms of this book) are often inextricably linked. When this is the case, I have joined them by an ampersand thus "Wealth **&** Esteem" but when I mean them as separate they are written as "Wealth **and** Esteem".

Skills

For both Life and Work Status, Skills are the abilities to perform tasks, to do jobs. For Skills to count they must be active and relevant to the Jobs they are applied to. An amateur conjurer's Life Skills are excellent at a child's birthday party but less so in singing the amateur tenor solo part in Bach's Magnificat. A garage mechanic, with his Work Skills, is just the man to service my car but less than the ideal person to operate on my brain. Skills, as well as needing relevance, are measured according to how important they are. Snow White is accepted into the Seven Dwarves' household because of her superiority over her hosts in terms of cooking and cleaning. For the dwarves, that is what mattered. That she was beautiful while they were ugly was of marginal importance to them, though I do sometimes wonder what made Happy so happy. (See Comparative Status 2.8 below).

Wealth

Work Wealth is income received from labour, commonly from wages or salaries, but includes other work-related remunerations to which a monetary value can be ascribed, such as pension remittals or health insurances.

Life Wealth is made up of all financial assets held by the individual, plus any other that is available from, for instance, those held by close family members. Thus, for example, a spouse's income from labour is his or her Work Wealth, but the value of their house is usually jointly held as their Life Wealth. Allocating Life Wealth between partners can, unfortunately, lead to considerable disagreement, particularly when it is an issue during divorce.

Wealth in itself and as a contributor to Esteem suffers from **the Law of Diminishing Returns**. Every addition to the pile is less effective than the one before. This fact does not occur to the very rich whose need for even more dosh than those less blessed is evident.

<u>Esteem</u>

Esteem is by far the most important element in both Work Status and Life Status. Indeed, in Maslow's Hierarchy of Needs, top of the pyramid goes to "Self Actualization", which is the drive to boost one's own esteem. The second layer of the pyramid is actually esteem itself, the regard that other people have of you. The remainder of psychological needs and basic needs are subordinate. "So Skills, Wealth and Status remain but the greatest of these is Esteem".

Work Esteem is that derived from your occupation, Life Esteem is that derived from all aspects of your existence other than that occupation. The domination of Esteem over the other elements of Status is easily exhibited: suppose ten managers were offered a new title of Director or an increase of 10% in salary. Nine out of ten would choose the enhanced title and the dissenter would probably have a gambling problem that needed satisfying.

## 2.4 Inter-Relationships Between Skills, Wealth and Esteem

For Life Status there is little pattern to the connections between the three elements if any at all. Usually Life Esteem is boosted by Life Wealth but Life Skills are valued for their own sake.

For Work Status, however, there is a clear bond and this is a key concept in this book: **Work Skills drive Work Wealth and Work Esteem.** To turn this around, increasing Work Wealth and Esteem are the **rewards** of increasing Work Skills.

Elements of Life and Work profiles can be interchanged. For example, a hobby (Life Skill) may become an occupation (Work Skill). Income (Work Wealth) is transferable to savings (Life Wealth). Work Esteem can provide a halo-effect on Life Esteem. That is why some celebrities are allowed to pontificate on things that they know less about than Joe Public.

Therefore, the above premise can be proved:

Life Skill + Work Skills = Total Skills

Life Wealth + Work Wealth = Total Wealth

Life Esteem + Work Esteem = Total Esteem

QED Life Status + Work Status = Total Status

For the remainder of this book we will usually be talking about Total Status concentrating on Work Status, but it is always sensible to remind ourselves of its dual make up.

It should be noted that the three elements of Status are not independent of each other; in particular Skills can reinforce Wealth and Esteem and Wealth can, on its own, reinforce Esteem. Similarly,

Esteem can produce Wealth, but these two are unlikely to help with Skills unless they, for instance, support a hobby.

Case Study:  Memphis Blues

A young lad is born in the US of A. Shall we christen him with the unusual name of Elvis?  He enjoys singing in his local gospel choir. He is a cherubic child and he is encouraged by the congregation in his singing talents. So much so that he attempts to make a profession of his vocal dexterity, and, after a few rebuffs, he is moderately successful in a burgeoning recording career.

A retired military man (shall we name him Colonel Parker?) takes a considerable interest in Elvis's proficiency and, for an immodest cut of future earnings, manages the rest of his life.

Elvis becomes the world's leading proponent of a certain type of popular minstrel songs; after a brief sojourn in his country's defence in foreign climes, he resumes his recording undertakings and adds acting in films to his many irons in the fire. His popularity is much magnified by his comeliness and an original form of solo gymnastics whilst performing his songs.

With what little is left of his earnings as allowed by the good Colonel, he purchases a modest property in Memphis Tennessee which he names after an area owned by an actor called Kelly.  Unfortunately, he puts on a little weight and becomes dependent on ill-advised medication.

After a few valedictory performances in the US of A Capital of Chance, he dies uncomfortably.

Commentary  Amateur Gospel to professional singing = transfer of Life Skills to Work Skills.

Work Skills establishes considerable Work Wealth and Esteem.

Acting performances add to Work Wealth without too much diminution of Work Esteem (Total Status marginally increased?)

Purchase of property = transfer of Work Wealth to Life Wealth.

It should be remembered that the changes in Status elements happened over Elvis's lifetime; that perspective should mitigate our own natural impatience. Unless you are lucky enough to inherit Wealth and, perhaps, Esteem, the chief way to build Status is through improving your Skills. Elvis is a great champion of this pattern, but you will observe that its effects are not permanent.

## 2.5  Time Aspects of Status

A reminder: the above case study illustrates an important point: all components of Status (Life Skills, Wealth and Esteem + Work Skills, Wealth and Esteem) and therefore Total Status, always vary with time.

This is a good place to look at the beginning and ending of Status. I contend that Status begins at birth with passable relevant Life Skills (ensuring being fed and cleansed on demand), OK Work Wealth if you're lucky (established savings accounts from grandparents) and significant but variable Life Esteem (screaming at 3am / what a beautiful baby!)

I also contend that Status usually ceases or at least diminishes with death. We can all think of many men and women whose reputation (Total Esteem) is greater now after their death than during their life. Indeed some martyrs seek to increase and crystalise their Total Esteem by seeking their own demise, but this is unusual and its effectiveness uncertain.

Case Study: Fine Dining

The familiar scene is a table for two in an expensive restaurant. The wine list, a tome about the size and weight of the Encyclopedia Britannica in Large Print, has been left discretely on the gentleman's side of the table. The food has been ordered and the Sommelier appears from nowhere. He has one of those little silver flat dishes hanging on a chain round his neck

Sommelier "Would Sir care to have some wine with his repast?"

Sir, "Yes please. It is not that easy to choose from such a big list. What would you recommend?

The Sommelier's eye glitter. "Of course, Sir. It would be my pleasure to assist. May I ask what you are eating?"

Sir, "My wife is having the scallops and the chicken, I the sole thing and then some beef."

Sommelier, "Ah. I see Sir's difficulty. Might I suggest a bottle of a dry white followed by a medium red?"

Sir, "Oh no. We don't drink much. We couldn't manage more than one bottle."

Sommelier, "Bien –sur, Monsieur." He takes back the list and pretends to read through with a deep frown on his visage. "Here we are, Sir. I think that number 321 would fit the bill."

The list is passed back with the 1963 Mouton Rothschild pointed to with a well- manicured finger.

Sir just manages to stifle his gasp. Summoning his courage and remembering who is the boss here he says sternly, "Oh no, that is far too expensive."

Sommelier, with a tiny sniff, "Of course, Sir." To the lady, "May I ask Madam if this is a special occasion?"

Madam, slightly embarrassed, "Yes, it's our wedding anniversary."

Sommelier, "Congratulations to you both! It is our pleasure to welcome you to our establishment to celebrate!"

The Sommelier pauses, waiting for Sir to change his mind. No luck.

Our Sommelier tries to take the list but Sir now sees what he thinks he is about and retains it and starts looking through in desperation. He chances on and orders, "We will have a bottle of number 142, please."

The Sommelier recovers his list and checks out the selection. "Ah yes, Sir." He glances around furtively to see if anyone is listening and leans in and, in a stage whisper, informs the couple, "A very good choice, if I may say so, Sir. I can see that you know your cabernet from your sauvignon. But, just between you and me, I think that your choice has become a slight jaded since you tried it last. I would avoid."

Madam who, naturally has not been invited into the chamber of secrets, says brightly, "Oh, go on, George, this is the only time we will celebrate our thirtieth."

Sir tries one last gambit, "Is 1963 a good year?"

Sommelier, "Dazzling, Sir, right at the top."

Sir, recognizing that he has lost a common battle, "Go on then. We only live once."

Sommelier, "You have made a very good choice, Sir. I am sure that you will find it, shall we say, a perfect accompaniment to a perfect meal on a perfect day."

After service has ended Sir and Madam, as they get into their limousine to drive home, spy the Sommelier (now out of his uniform and dressed in sweatshirt and jeans), dodging out of the back door of the restaurant into the alley and scrabbling on foot and through the rain to the bus stop. He spies his erstwhile guests as they swish pass.

Commentary  Who do you think has the higher Status in this exchange? The Sommelier claims higher Skills (relative to the task), Sir has higher Wealth as he is paying (over the odds) and each would claim higher Esteem (from Sir's point of view, the Sommelier is working for him, from the Sommelier's point of view the roles are reversed).

Whatever, the perspectives of Status change dramatically with the mutual sightings after dinner. No matter how low your Status is today, it will probably be better tomorrow. Similarly, you may be at the top now but there is "many a slip between cup and lip".

By the by, you will have noticed that claret was probably the worst choice to accompany the food and 1963 was a disaster for Mouton.

This leads us nicely into:

## 2.6  Perspectives of Status

To his friends, a "paragon of animals", to his enemies the devil incarnate. To the police officer, a probable felon, to his congregation their spiritual leader. To her king a subject, to her staff a prince. To his dog the master, to her cat the maid. To his young son a soccer wizard, to his older daughter a dancing embarrassment. To his mother a bad marriage, to his wife a mistaken marriage.

Much like Schrodinger's cat, Status only exists by observation and each observer has a different perspective. There is **no absolute** and the chimera shifts and turns with the seasons.

Whose perspective is the most important of course changes with who does the observing and is particularly relevant in distinctions between Life and Work Statuses. Your boss is little concerned with your family life and your family is often only concerned with the Wealth element of your work.

A common problem is that perspectives of Status can appear to be wrong (as Mark Twain's Prince and the Pauper each discovered); this is a false assumption since there is no **absolute "right" Status** for anyone, so ideas of "right" and "wrong" are in any existential terms misleading.

Case Study:  Brand Blindness

A teenager (male) has scrimped and saved and has gathered together, without stealing from his mother's purse for once, sufficient funds to purchase a designer T shirt. Naturally he is very keen to demonstrate his new acquisition and hurries to a rearranged meeting with his girlfriend.

Impressions are that girlfriend is enthralled with the T shirt and, as a corollary, with the teenager himself; this opinion is formed from her facial expressions and demonstrations of affection rather that her speech as she talks in a language which, though similar to English, is not familiar.

After a few weeks the teenager takes off the T shirt and places it in the home receptacle indicating that it requires washing. His Mother wisely reads the cleaning instructions before washing to discover that it is labelled "Dry Clean Only" which requires an expenditure of time and money from her and not her son.

Commentary As is far from unusual, the perspectives of the teenager's Life Esteem are considerably different between his girlfriend and his mother. He himself will side with his girlfriend since that perspective coincides with his own; anyway, that is what mothers are for. Understanding that people think differently to you about the Status of others (and, importantly, about your own) is a major aptitude and is key to utilising Employment Plots as I outline later.

## 2. 7 Self Awareness

If any perspective of Status comes close to an absolute it is a person's own evaluation of his or her profiles. Unlike the myriad versions of the circumspections of others, one's own regard is relatively adamantine. It is like a diamond which is cut and polished throughout the lifetime but always remains a gem and thus a thing of beauty. Despite this, you should know that you are not the best driver or lover in the world; I am.

An academic study has introduced us to the Dunning-Krugger Effect which, in essence, sets out that people hold a higher view of their own status than that recorded by others. Perhaps yet another academic study, no doubt at someone's expense, which proves the bleedin' obvious. Habitually, it is easier to attempt to modify others' perspectives of your Status than it is to change your own mind.

We are all exceptional in our own regard! There are unusual cases where a person's own view of his or her status is lower than that of others. The first is where the person suffers a mental illness like **depression**. This is not funny.

The second is usually confined to young children as regards their parents or a special circumstance involving two adults. This is called **Love** and is usually temporary. It is funny.

It is often said that the ability to realistically distinguish between your own Status as you see it and that as perceived by someone else is a very good thing. I am not sure about that: when people are wrong they should be corrected.

"O was some power the giftie gie us to see ourselves as ithers see us" (*Robert Burns*).

Case Study:  Trouble in the Orient

The owner of a business decides to create an agency in Japan and, having set up a meeting with a prospective company, she visits that country. As is usual, her Japanese potential business partners take her to a karaoke bar after dinner. She misunderstands the alcoholic strength of sake (who doesn't?) and demonstrates what she considers her considerable stentorian voice to the assembled company. To that audience the performance is not a success; she interprets the stunned silence following her singing as reverence. Much worse, she had not taken care before arrival in Japan to study and learn the distinctive mores and required manners in Japan and she seriously offends her hosts. They also discover that her business consists of her and her brother's wife and is nowhere near the scale that was worth any effort. The evening is not a success.

Commentary  The businesswoman's Status takes a big hit with her Japanese hosts with Life Skill and Esteem, Work Skills and Wealth all taking a battering. For the woman herself all is tickety-boo with, for her, enhanced Life Skills and Esteem with possible doubts on Work Esteem when they pack her into a taxi and she never hears from them again. If you occasionally take the trouble to reflect on how your Status appears to others you will only benefit; such detective efforts are easier than you might think.

## 2.8 Comparative Status

There is no such thing as absolute Status – **every person's level is determined when compared and contrasted with someone else's**. These judgements are dependent on the situation in which they are made: the CEO is supreme in his company but is the hacker in his Sunday four-ball at the golf club. This idea of comparative Status is important for our prospects in Work!

Case Study: But I am Better than You at ...

A "journalist" works for a small local newspaper. He somehow drifted into the job having started straight from school as the tea boy. His main source of copy is to be found in his local law courts where the unfortunates of this world have their fates decided.

For every story, he seeks the most negative aspects. He lies to and cheats his informants with absolutely no care as to their lives. He has no family to advise him. His only skill is fiddling his expenses, which his editor is fully aware of but compensates for with a pitiful salary. His spelling and grammar are appalling, and his copy is only saved from serious error by the office word processor. He regularly gets the names and other details of his interviewees wrong. He takes long lunches and his colleagues all think that his daily excess alcohol consumption is a major cause of his bad work performance and ethic. He is already on two verbal and one written warning about his performance and inevitably, when the next one occurs, he will be sacked. Both he and the newspaper have been served legal papers and are being sued for libel following one of his whoppers. This subject has virtually no skills. Even a teaboy has more. No savings, no family, no future. His editor and work and colleagues despise him and only tolerate him because no one else can be found to do the job.

<u>Commentary</u> And one other big reason to tolerate him: they all look much better by comparison. The one thing that keeps us sane in our competitive world is knowing that someone else is worse off than we are. It is probably true that the lower Status we have the more we depend on comparing ourselves with those with inferior standing (and vice versa).

Comparisons of Status are of two forms: **Selective** and **Universal**. Simply put, I can compare my clarinet playing (Grade 2 failed) selectively with others in my amateur orchestra but also universally with all the clarinet players in the world.

## 2.9  Society and Its Influence on Status

Different societies place different emphasis on the three elements of Status. For instance:

In Renaissance Italy Skills were rated much more than in our current culture. This appreciation was not confined to the Arts but included more mundane occupations. Guilds (cf. Trades Unions) were established to nurture and promote those Skills.

In India and other nations there is a very strong caste system. Your birth and parentage are more important than Wealth. Your employment is dictated by your caste and is an unusual case of Esteem determining Skills.

In communist regimes Esteem is dependent on Esteem.

In capitalist civilisations Wealth is the key determinant of Esteem.

## 2.10 Communicating Status

Whatever the society, Status is nothing unless it is communicated to the others in the hierarchy. We even check our Self Awareness for imaginary evaluations by others to be smugly nurtured.

Case Study:  At the Barbecue

A barbecue party is in full swing at a venue in the Hamptons, New York and a conversation occurs between two strangers just introduced:

A "Hi, buddy, how ya doing?

B "Great, thanks. Where ya from?"

A "Oak Plains, Nevada. What ya earn?"

B "Around $250,000 plus Lincoln Town car, company Amex and insurances"

A "That's impressive. What do you have to do to get that?"

B "Top Sales Manager for BigCorp the last three years running. Got to work hard if you want to run your own sailboat and support the kids at Harvard. What's your trade?"

 A "I'm just here to clean the pool"

Commentary Often a direct approach to communicating Status has much to recommend it and it can become habitual in certain societies. Note B's quick and effective statements to provide information on his Life and Work Skills (sailing, top sales), Life and Work Wealth (sailboat, income) and Life and Work Esteem (kids at top university, highly rated employee).  A, realising the fight is already lost, does not waste time communicating any competition.

Compare and contrast with a similar conversation on the other side of the pond:

Case Study:  At Another Barbecue

The scene is a barbecue party at a country estate. Two gentlemen converse:

A "Have you come far?"

B "No, not really. We are neighbours of the Andersons. We came over in the wife's little car."

A "How do you come to know them?"

B "Oh, we go way back. My wife is godmother to little Jamie, but fortunately that doesn't take up too much of her valuable time!"

A "Enjoying yourself?"

B "Very much. It is so nice to get away from the office."

A "Been away anywhere nice for your holidays?"

B "We don't get much opportunity. We did manage a little break at our regular spot down South. Our daughter managed to "come down" to be with us."

A "Nice food and drink?"

B "Absolutely.  I didn't know that Proseccos are getting really rather good these days. What line of business are you in?"

A" Oh, I don't have to work. My wife is a top model. She is over there just out of the pool. (With a wink) Centre of attention as always!  She knows how to look after me."

End of game.

Commentary Indirect communication of Status can be done just as efficiently as more direct methods and can contain more information.

In the above conversation, B succeeds in relaying the following messages:

> Our estate is the same size as that of our host.
>
> My wife has a Ferrari. I indulge her. She is grateful.
>
> We are first on the guest list, not afterthoughts.
>
> My wife is an asset.
>
> We are church goers, which we think is a good thing.
>
> On our holidays, we are not common tourists.
>
> We own a property, probably in the South of France. It is staffed.
>
> "Come down" means the daughter is at Oxford or Cambridge University.
>
> Champagne is my usual drink. Prosecco is for plebs like you.

Whether you go for direct or more indirect communication of your Status depends on the circumstances and, in particular, your audience. B's conversation in the Hamptons would be regarded as counterproductive in more so-called "civilised" societies, whereas his compatriot from one of those societies would express nothing whatsoever of his Status over the pond. In fact he would be considered a ****.

## 2.11 Techniques for Communicating Status: Boasting

There are many techniques commonly utilised to communicate Status to others and we can consider four of the most common:

**Boasting** is the verbal expression of your Status; its advantage is that it is straightforward, direct and, if used properly, unlikely to be misinterpreted.

However, the advisability of Boasting as a procedure is very much dependent on societal norms. In the Case Study above, B in the Hamptons, it is well within his custom and manners because the etiquette in his country both allows and encourages his exchanges with A.

The permissibility of boasting is also dependent on the expertise promoted. The rule is that the more trivial the topic, the more license is allowed. Thus, outside of the Hamptons, affluence is a definite no-no. The success of your wonderful children is about in the middle of acceptability. Your personal weather forecast is OK everywhere.

The big temptation in boasting is to overstate any element of your Status. The downsides and dangers of being caught out are severe and a careful balance needs to be achieved between likelihood and unfeasibility. This is often referred to as the "Emperor's New Clothes" syndrome.

## 2.12: Techniques for Communicating Status: Conspicuous Consumption

A major contributor to the science of Status communication was Thorstein Veblen, a much under-appreciated economist writing at the turn of the nineteenth and twentieth centuries. In his seminal work (*Thorstein Veblen "The Theory of the Leisure Class", Macmillan 1899*) he traces the history of what he calls "pre-potence over others" from tribal through feudal to industrial societies where merit and economic utility are now communicated though **"Conspicuous Consumption"**. Every aspect of our demeanor and behaviour signifies our Status either overtly or unconsciously. In his inspirational Chapter "Dress as an Expression of the Pecuniary Culture" Veblen shows how the Leisure Class use dress to demonstrate their lack of need to work through their attire.

Conspicuous Consumption more generally is a demonstration of status through expenditure and asset retention well beyond normal needs; the further from those needs the better.

Case Study:  Top of the Pile?

Vladimir is an "oligarch" in a totalitarian state. How he reached this comfortable position is through the usual route: best buddies with the state's President with a good scratch-my-back-and-I-will scratch-yours friendship. He made his first billions in oil and gas, moved on to steel production and then to banking, where he was especially useful.

He has moved his abodes from the totalitarian state to libertarian Europe, where his bribery is better appreciated and there is little competition compared with what he would find in the Americas. Any trivial problems in life are easily dealt with either by his private militia or by a simple call to his premier. As long as he keeps up the kickbacks then all is hunky-dory. From his looks alone you can tell that he is as thick as two short bricks but do not tell him that or else the bricks might take a close look at your face. Despite his unbecoming demeanor,    Vladimir's possessions are grotesque by any normal standards and are based on his misunderstanding of value. His many houses are decorated in the Louis Quinze style (give or take a Louis) with an abundance of gold; his many cars are all personalised to a ridiculous degree and he gnaws his fingernails to the quick in his angst that his "yacht" is only the fourth biggest in the world. He encourages his divorces as the resulting publicity advertises his fortune. As set out above, the Law of Diminishing Returns means that Vladimir can never be satisfied with what he has and incremental Wealth adds nothing to his Esteem. My heart bleeds.

He is feared but not otherwise respected. Not even for his vast riches. The feelings are mutual - he doesn't care for me much, either.

Commentary Vladimir's mistake (no, I am not envious) is to equate the joys of mammon with prestige. He confuses, more than most, his own perception of Status with that of others.

His Conspicuous Consumption impresses his hangers-on but is ridiculed by the envious.

Rest assured that everyone has your Wealth down to a T. You do not have to publicise the notional value of your house; the whole world already knows. Same for your car. Same for the holidays you take. Do not over-egg your consumption by making it too conspicuous.

## 2.13  Techniques for Communicating Status : False Modesty

The contrary technique to communicate Status is called **False Modesty** where you downplay your Status levels. A good example is that provided by B in the Case Study above: the reference to "my wife's little car" is meant to imply her possession of a serious and expensive vehicle. Much depends on the social norms that understand this deceit so it should work in the environment of a country estate but could be misinterpreted somewhere else. Just in case, visual clues are often provided to communicate that the technique is being utilized such as a comedy cough or a wink.

Case Study: Superstar!

Clark Kent is a good example of where a Work Profile is much less important than his Life Profile but he keeps this very quiet. Workwise he is a reporter for the Daily Planet periodical in the city of Metropolis and has good parentage (foster), a Mr. and Mrs. Kent, from whom he inherited his excellent work ethic. He was brought up in Smallvillle, Kansas. His Life profile is much more interesting and comes to the fore when he, in an arrangement with AT&T, transforms himself into Superman (his stage name).

Love interest is provided by a fellow journalist, a Lois Lane who blows hot and cold depending on how Clark dresses.

His parents brought him up to be a vigilante and to fight crime where has a 100% success record. In these many pursuits he changes his character from dreary Clark to flashy Superman. He dons special clothing which never needs cleaning so that he can wear his underpants on the outside. His vision problems as Clark (he wears spectacles) disappear when he makes this change, which is a good thing because his new uniform does not have any pockets to keep them in. His Skills as Superman are excellent, with extraordinary strength and the ability to fly. Generally, the criminals whom he overcomes, after a wide range of difficulties, are various, but he does often encounter one consistent opponent, a Mr. Lex Luther. From these encounters, it is clear that our Lois is stringing Clark along. Whenever Superman appears, she is all over him and acts as if the over developed muscles of Superman are all a girl could ask for. He, however, will not go beyond the light petting stage with Lois or any other girl and there is a small question mark concerning cross-dressing.

We must talk about Kryptonite. This substance is easily found in Superman's neck of the woods (and, probably, China) but it is unusual to lay hands on it elsewhere. Kryptonite has a peculiar effect on Superman akin to him being very drunk. This effect is always temporary however, so we can put it on one side. Other than that, his talents are right at the top where we also find his significant Esteem. It is hard to think of anyone with anything like his Skills; he would make an awesome quarterback if he were entered into the draft. It is a bit more difficult to explain his rock bottom Wealth: anyone else with anything like his talents would use them to bolster his earnings from the miserable salary as a failing journalist but this never seems to bother him. He could very easily break into Fort Knox and get away with it. Think on, Superman is not the only person whose Skill and Esteem are so high that they can choose to forego Wealth and the world is a better place as a result.

Commentary Clark is the epitome of False Modesty. It is beyond me and everyone why he does not boast of his many talents. He must be able to do better than Lois. His problem is the common one with this method: no one understands the joke. The many hints that he provides, especially to Lois, do not land on fertile soil because he exaggerates his reporter profile to such an extent that no one could possibly think that he was the city's great protector.

The lesson is that False Modesty is a dangerous practice: too easily misconstrued and, when employed and comprehended, irritating.

## 2.14 Techniques in Communicating Status : Labels

Our fourth common technique used to communicate Status is the application of **labels.** Because much Status communication is subtle with significant opportunity for misunderstanding, most societies have developed a system where labels are attached to names to make Status obvious and less efficient methods superfluous. In commercial organisations labels as such as "CEO" or "President" are top of the list. Elsewhere a system of "Honours" is extant, seen best in the United Kingdom with titles such as "OBE" or "Knight/Dame" which are scattered like confetti. These sobriquets are highly desirable and usually require a significant investment (for the lower trophies e.g. much work for a charity) or cash (for the higher trophies e.g. donations to a political party). The upper echelon of the honours system (e.g. Dukes/Duchesses, Prince/Princesses) are extremely rare but somewhat tarnished by the lack of effort needed to obtain them. Outside of those peculiar circumstances, having the right parents establishes Status from the beginning.

At the end of the day, if all else fails then the method of last resort is to shout "DO YOU KNOW WHO I AM?"

## 2.15  Vicarious Status

Lower Status persons often attempt to increase perceptions of that Status by piggy-backing onto another's. Common forms are:

Of the family –

"My wife is a top gynaecologist" (NB All gynaecologists are top gynaecologists)

"My Dad is tougher than your Dad"

"My cousin's wife's uncle's brother in law is a bishop"

Amongst friends –

"I often get invited to the Director's box in the stadium by ?? "

"I am great buddies with ?? "

"?? says she cannot live without my yoga classes"

With strangers –

"That's me in the photo with  ?? "

"I had a one night stand with ?? He says it was the best night of his life. I wonder if he remembers me?"

"'Ere. You know what? Guess who I had in the back of my cab last week?"

Claiming Vicarious Status is only activated when the Status referred to is understood to be above that of the person doing the claiming.

You are unlikely to hear:

"My old man's a dustman, he wears a dustman's hat!"

"My brother is a burglar" (Unless his Wealth Status over-compensates for lack of Esteem).

"I actually enjoy commuting to work by train."

The most important and everyday form of Vicarious Status for an individual is to join a team where you can contribute to and share Work and Life Skills, Wealth and Esteem with the team and benefit and contribute to those of your peers.

Case Study:  An Introduction to Football

Football (aka Soccer) is a game in name only between two "teams" of ten "players" plus a spare. They "play" the game on a "pitch" and the size of this pitch determines how much the players will earn. Your opponents are called "the opposition" but often something else by "fans" who, believe it or not, actually pay to watch and shout.

Each end of the pitch for professional players has a "goal", a space with netting at the back and sides. The object of the game is to place a "ball" into the net without using your hands. This is called "scoring" and is not to be confused with obtaining illicit substances. The players leave that till after the game.

Each team is divided into three groups of players: "Forwards" who have the highest Esteem and are paid the most, "Midfielders" who are next in ranking, and lastly "Full Hacks" who are in the lowest echelon. Sometimes the team will have a "Striker" who, as the name implies, stands around on his or her own not doing any work.

The forwards' job is to get paid for advertising inappropriate products and, because they are nearest the opposition's goal they have the best chance of scoring. The full hack's job is to kick anything that moves on the pitch. The rest of their team know who their full hackers are so know how to avoid them. The midfielders are confused but spend most of the time hiding from full hackers of either team.

The numbers in each group varies for three reasons. Firstly the "Manager" (who is definitely not in the team but gets to go on television or the radio) talks about a "system" which pretends to instruct the players about where they should stand on the pitch, communicated by hieroglyphics on a blackboard before the game; this is always deliberately ignored by the players because they never understand them. Secondly, all the midfielders and the full hacks want to increase their earnings so use every opportunity to play the role of the forwards and get advertising contracts. Thirdly, none of the fans can tell what the system is supposed to be but this does not stop them offering for consideration, alternative systems to those of the manager, together with suitable admiring epithets. The manager dances at the side of the pitch to bask in this approbation.

Right at the back of the ten players and in front of his or her net is a spare player who is not in the team: the "goalie". They are not allowed to wear the team uniform (the "Strip") and have one all of their own to help distinguish them from the team. Their job is to pick the ball out of the net when the opposition scores and to shout and swear at their squad. In compensation they are allowed a few goes at kicking the ball a long way into the opposite net, almost universally failing - though it has been known to be achieved, which is why they keep trying.

All the players except the goalie have a bath or shower together making loud complaints about him or her. This is designed to establish "Team Spirit". Should one of the players have scored a goal (unlikely) then they are expected to present themselves to be interviewed by the media, best done before the ablutions whilst still in the team kit, thus marketing it.

Commentary  Each player in the team has individual Status, often very high, with some level of Skills but often massive Wealth & Esteem beyond all sense. Together with this, there is a bonus of Status from being part of a team, which is in addition to the aggregate of them all. The goalie is not part of the team and thus is excluded from that Vicarious Status.

Playing your part in a team is, if done properly, a useful method to gain Status vicariously by stealing the achievements of other team members. You need to bear in mind, however, that your team-mates are after your successes. The name of the game is to put as little in as possible while taking the maximum out. Because this is very competitive, team building is a staple of all Management development courses where tutors observe teams in action to pinch their ideas.

In theory, Vicarious Status is less valuable than that directly earned but, at the margin, every little helps.

## 2.16  Work/Life Balance

Maintaining a good equilibrium between Life and Work Statuses is a constant challenge. Most of the time the efforts in doing so are subconscious but, when circumstances change, they can jump into focus. This often occurs during a period called a "Mid Life Crisis".

Case Study:  The Jobs Dilemma

A lady is offered a big promotion at work. Unfortunately this will involve more travel and more nights away from the family home. She is in a dilemma as to whether or not to take the job.

Commentary What should she, and her husband, do? They will give much conscious thought to making the decision but they probably will not realise that it will be based on her Status options and, to a lesser extent, how changes there will affect his Vicarious Status. She will reflect on her lower Life Skills and Esteem but higher Work Skills, Wealth and Esteem. The process of weighing up the "Work/Life Balance" is part of the means and not the end. Society mores will be important: where family life is central the decision will go one way, in a pecuniary culture it will go the other.

This, I think, is the right time to bring up the subject of Job Satisfaction, an oxymoron in my experience but said by other experts to exist. I suppose, for the sake of argument, that some people get a certain fulfilment from their occupation and it would be remiss of me if I did not include this hypothetical idea in this book.

Please stay with me whilst we consider it. Should Job Satisfaction exist then it contributes to Work Self Esteem and little else with no compensating impact on other aspects of Total Status.  I am willing to concede that publicising this unusual quality of employment could add to other's perspective of your Esteem but I expect the general response would be cynicism and envy, not approbation.

## 2.17  Status and Morality

The elements of Status and thus their aggregation have no morals or ethics in themselves. Skills are neither good nor bad, their quality is only dependent on their applicability. Wealth has no virtue, it is merely a means to an end, which may or may not be righteous. Esteem, in the normal course of events, carries with it a suggestion of honour. In this definition of Status (in this book i.e. not status as prestige in the real world) it signifies no value.

## 2.18  Conclusions and Chapter's Key Points

**When two or more humans (and animals) meet they always form a hierarchy**

**A person's Status is the measure used in establishing their place in a hierarchy**

**Status has two components: Work Status and Life Status**

**Both components have three elements: Skills, Wealth and Esteem**

**Status varies with time and is subject to different perspectives**

**Status has no absolute value but is used for comparisons**

**Communicating one's Status is a key talent in Work and Life**

# CHAPTER 3  INTRODUCING PICTOGRAMS and CAREER PATHS

## 3.1  Introduction

Only kidding about the exam!

I now want to introduce you to the next stages in putting together Employment Plots, the analytical tool for exploring different organisations and our role in them. We will, from now on, concentrate on **Work Status** and its part in Employment.

First off is the description of a basic pictogram which drafts Status against time. Secondly, we will introduce the concept of Career Paths - which are drawn on to the basic pictogram.

## 3.2  Graphics

The second stage in the manufacture of our diagnostic tool, the Employment Plot, uses a pictogram which compares Work Status as it develops over time.

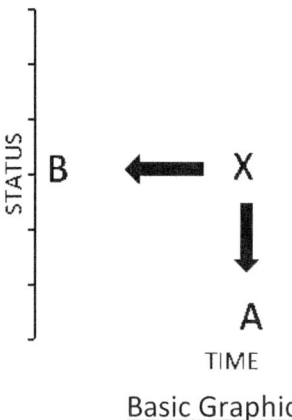

Basic Graphic

These **Plots** are **Models.** In the figure 3.2 "X" marks the spot which represents a level of Status "B" at a time "A".

You will remember that my Employment Plots (and this framework of them) are my inventions and act as the device to set out my General Theory of Organisations. In **every** plot from now on the normal Y axis shows Total Status for the subject discussed and the normal X axis shows Time.

## 3.3  Career Paths

At this, the third stage of building an Employment Plot, we can draw a **Career Path** on to our pictogram:

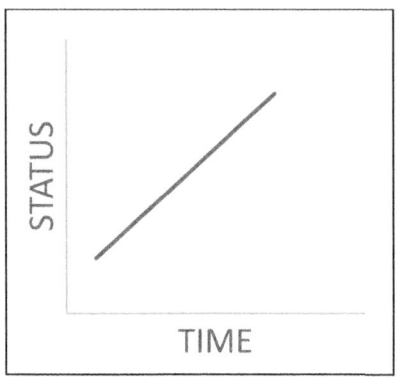

Model Career Path

Remembering Y = Status and X = Time, this plot shows a Career Path in the abstract for an individual. It shows increasing **Skills** over the time period. You will have observed that I have measured Skills rather than Status on the Y axis; bear with me on this and all will become clear. I also ask you to delay asking an obvious question: "what is the timeframe for the Career Path?", also to follow!

Meanwhile you will probably accept that, for Work Status Profiles, Skills will be the dominant element in their levels and Skills and Status are just about equivalent.

Clearly actual careers are much more complicated than this simple depiction; every actual career will have a wriggly line. Career Paths in the pictograms are constructs to illustrate general idea of a Career rather than an actual one, and the Case Studies that follow are **sketches** rather than histories.

To distinguish my Careers and their Paths from actual real careers I have started them with a capital "C".

## 3.4 Classes of Career Paths

Career Paths for you, me and everyone can have different start points and end points and their shape is defined accordingly. They show the development of Skills (as part of Status) over time for everyone. Remember the Golden Rules of Skills: a Career Path is ephemeral in itself and only has real value when used in a Comparison with other Paths. With these provisions I would like to group all types of Career Paths into three Classes: A = Inclined. B = Level and C = Declined.

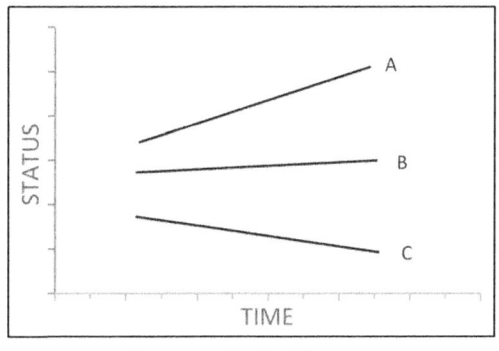

Career Path Classes

Class A (Inclined) is the type that we all aspire to: Growing Skills over our working lifetime.
Class B (Level) covers a multitude of situations where an individual labours in the same job all their working life with no increase in Skills.
Class C (Declining) shows the unfortunate record for an individual with reducing Skills.

The Peter Principle (the Special Theory) applies only to Class A Careers as they are hierarchical. By broadening the scope of our consideration to **all** types of Careers we can investigate a more comprehensive pool of livelihoods and expand our analysis into a General Theory.

Following are examples at **three different levels** (low, medium and high) within **each of the three Classes** so that we can get the overall idea of those different types.

## 3.5 Class 1: Inclined Career Paths

Case Study:  Steep Incline, Low Start and High Finish

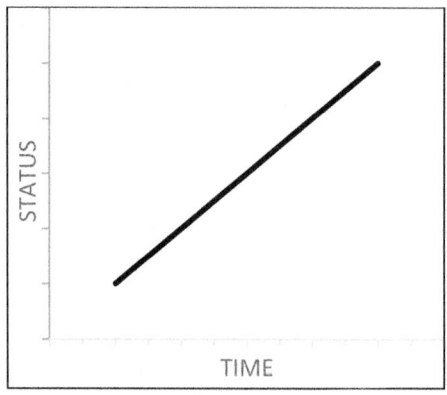

Steep Inclined Career Path

Thomas Cromwell came into this world in 1485 to a pretty poor family; he was not a gentleman born. His father was a drunken blacksmith who abused his son. His Career began early earning small titbits and showing impressive nascent skills. He spent quite a long time abroad but then returned to become a general factotum to Cardinal Wolsey where he grew in Wealth and Esteem big time. He stood by when the Cardinal's  head was chopped off so he could move onwards and upwards by playing Catherine of Aragon off against Anne Boleyn, choosing against Anne by arranging to have her head chopped off.

By now he was very chummy with King Henry 8 who was top dog in sixteenth century England, and he then continued his Career development by becoming especially useful to the King and dissing his friends, notably Thomas More, and arranging for their heads to be cut off.

Cromwell rose right to the top by becoming Master Secretary (more important than twenty first century secretaries) but then made the big big mistake of wildly exaggerating the charms of Anne of Cleves, thereby tricking the King into marrying the lady who turned out to be not what he was hoping for. In 1540 Henry therefore arranged for Cromwell's head to be chopped off.

Commentary  Thomas is a super example of Skills growing from the very small to the summit. What Mr. Cromwell teaches us is that you never know where your Career is going to take you. Although you think that you, with your Skill set, are headed along a particular road with foreseeable vocational outcomes, your Skills will be applicable to many different work situations.

The trick is to be open-minded as regards your future and not let the past determine what is yet to come.

Two words of warning. I do not recommend that you imitate Thomas in utilizing assassination as a means of Career progression as the outcome can most often turn out to be the opposite of that intended. Secondly, if you aspire to a Steeply Inclined Career you should remember that the slope is very precipitous and greasy and it is easy to fall off.

Case Study:  Medium Incline, Medium Start and Finish

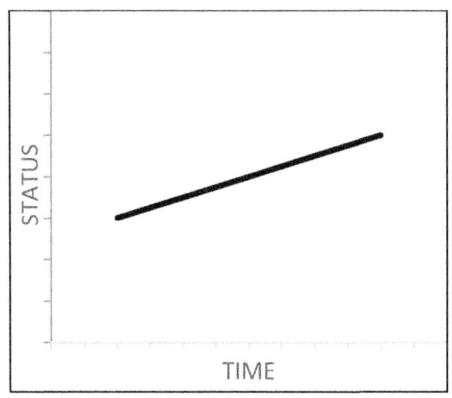

Medium Inclined Career Path

A go-getting Assistant Marketing Manager arrives at an airport and checks in for her flight. After going through security with practised and admirable forbearance, and completing the marathon through the Duty Free without being seduced by all the fake offers, she lands up at the news stand. She realizes that she has left her copy of The Wealth of Nations at home so she needs something to read on her flight. Within moments she spies, in the remainders section, a book on careers, occupation and organisations which is cheap enough that she can simply throw it away as the plane lands.

Oh Fortune! Within the first few pages she is catapulted into a deep understanding and realization of her own, her boss's and her colleague Assistant Marketing Managers' qualities and faults, reinforced as she gallops through the book, her eyes widening as she goes. Transfixed she even accepts the one free drink offered by the stewardess (even though she does not drink on Fridays) and does not fret about her neighbour taking up all of their joint armrest.

Back at work she immediately applies the myriad lessons learnt from the slim but densely argued volume and works assiduously to improve her prospects amongst her work peers and boss and even with her husband.
As you will have guessed, success is immediate and her continued application of the tenets absorbed drive her up her company's ladder for the remainder of her Career. She keeps the book and recommends it to all and sundry!

Commentary   From a Medium Skills Career start our Assistant Marketing Manager progresses smoothly to higher positions. By improving her Skills from studying the Status characteristics of relevant work colleagues and family and, in particular their perspective of her, she is in a great position to demonstrate her aptitude to progress up the ladder.

The lesson is that we should not be too passive in our Career development. It is too easy to sit back and complain that we are not progressing fast enough. By researching around your immediate role as widely as you can manage you will be in a better place to take advantage when those opportunities do arise. You have already made a good start by acquiring this book, but do not expect any further reading to come anywhere near this for insights and perspicacity!

Case Study: Small Incline, High Start and Finish

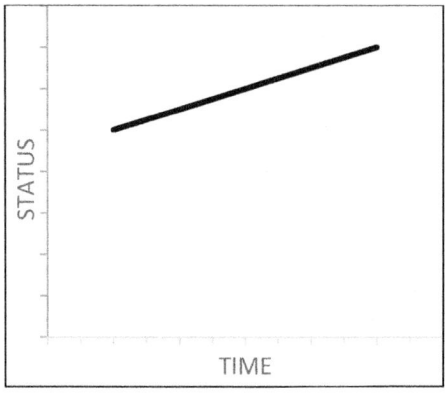

Small Inclined Career Path

Nelson Mandela (1918 – 2013) lived in a twentieth century society in which the population divided into a majority and an elite. The elite minority held the capital, the majority supplied the cheap labour which the elite utilized efficiently. The elite wanted to go further in their domination by living their lives as separately as possible from that of the majority. Yes, this society existed and its vestiges still do. This, for once, is not a fairy tale.

Nelson campaigned against this system all his life, so effectively that the elite threw him into prison for twenty years. On his release he continued his crusade with growing success, eventually becoming the country's President. Like all well balanced statesmen the right thought him too lefty and the left too righty. He was awarded the Nobel Peace Prize, shared with Frederik Willem de Klerk, a member of the elite who considerably helped Nelson and definitely earned his share of the prize. Nelson abandoned his special Skills in rock-breaking and put them aside as childish things.

Commentary   Nelson's story is a good example of different perspectives of Skills and how they can change over time resulting in different Career Paths. The perception of these Skills amongst the majority grew slowly but steadily from his royal family background, through his work to bring about a more equal society, to his most revered title of "Madiba" (= father). This regard for his Skills amongst the majority was joined in later life by the high respect of the elite. The Wealth and Esteem from the Nobel Prize also helped a bit.

The message is this: sometimes in your working life (and outside of work) it is possible that you believe in something (which you have the Skills to achieve) so strongly that you are willing to sacrifice Wealth and Esteem to help achieve it.

Nelson's Career Path reflects the perspective of the majority in his society; that of the minority would be very different (low start, eventually high finish.)

Many people hold jobs where they are dedicated to things that, in their mind, benefit society rather than themselves. They are willing to forgo Wealth, and the Esteem of others, for Self Esteem. That furrow is often a lonely one and society, rather than being grateful, will attempt to lure you back to their norms. Consider carefully before you embark.

## 3.6 Class Two: Level Career Paths

We now turn to our three examples of Level Career Paths.

Case Study: Level Career Path, Low Level

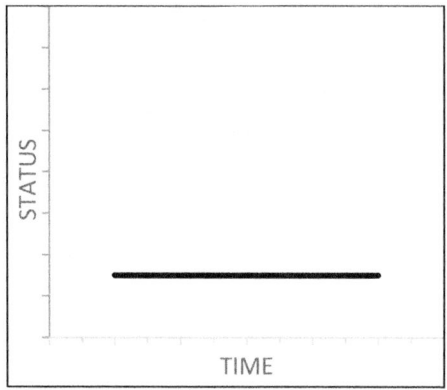

Level Career Path, Low Level

Mrs. Gently has a neighbour who has a dog. The neighbour thinks that his dog is wonderful: good with his children, always wears a happy and faithful expression, sleeps through the night and sees off other dogs in the park. The neighbour is especially proud of the dog's tricks such as "shake a paw" and "roll over" which the dog will perform only in expectation of a doggy treat which is always available.

Mrs. Gently is less enamoured of the canine. As far as she is concerned he has been a nightmare since he entered the neighbour's establishment as a puppy. He (the dog, not the neighbour) gets through a hole in their joint fence to do his business in her garden, he (the dog, not the neighbour) howls when nobody else is in the house, molts and spreads the residue all over when he jumps up on her, does not walk to heel, fights every other dog in the vicinity, terrorizes the cat and casts a meaningful eye over

Mrs. Gently's ankles when they unavoidably meet. She would prefer he (the neighbour) spent the money she regards as wasted on the dog's food and treats on mending the hole in the fence. When Mrs. Gently has taken an opportunity to discuss the dog's behavior with her adversaries (the neighbour and the dog) it is as if they are talking to each other in different languages.

Commentary  Our canine has a low Career Path according to Mrs. Gently. This is a good illustration of perspectives of Skills that are poles apart. The dog is not a sheepdog or any good as a guard dog so we are looking here at the dog's Low Level Life Skills and Career Path. Perspectives on Skills can differ widely, as we know.

The neighbour thinks his dog has high Life Skills:  Mrs. Gently thinks otherwise: although she talks about her desire for the dog to be put down she doesn't mean it. She just wishes the neighbour, the dog (or preferably both) moved house.

Within your organization there will be, very likely, someone who you think is useless and a pain but who does not suffer from general opprobrium. Step back and review: the majority opinion should be considered over-riding. Why is it that you are at odds with the mainstream? The beam in your eye outweighs the many motes of others. Even if you continue with your beliefs it is best to keep quiet about them. You should also consider that there will be one, if not more, in your company who think that you are the dog. Our hound is insensible to his Career Path and you may be too.

Case Study: Level Career Path, Medium Level

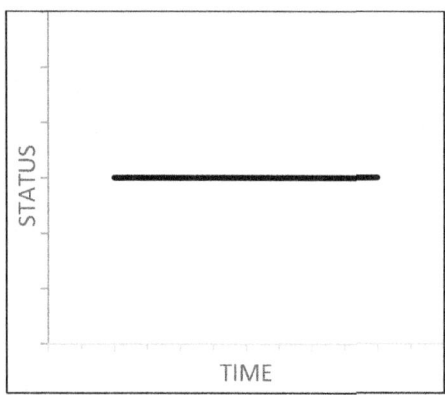

Level Career Path, Medium Level

Satan (aka The Devil, Lucifer) universally has a bad press. The one exception is of an odd cabal of the populace called Satanists, but they are few and far between and have the reputation of being a bit strange.

Putting the Satanists aside, Satan would figure in most lists of baddies, even worse than Hitler, Genghis Khan, Attila the Hun and that one on the television – you know who I mean!

Things started pretty well in his life, being a top bod in the angels' hierarchy, but he made a category error by rebelling against God and was cast out of heaven. Since then he has fought a losing battle with everyone and everything in all the monotheistic religions especially Judaism, Christianity and Islam.

Satan's modus operandi is to offer his prospective clients significant powers and/or money in exchange for a one-off future payment of their soul. It is not known how many accept this buy now pay later scheme since the contracts are always confidential. One treaty to break this omerta was that between Satan and Adam and Eve, where Satan dressed up as a snake. Reading between the lines these two got very little for an apple which wasn't even ripe. It just goes to show how sneaky he is and that it is always best to be on one's guard, since he comes in many tempting forms and he does not need to pull the snake trick more than once.

Commentary You will ask how someone so universally reviled gets a medium Career Path with mid-range Skills. Upon reflection you have to admit that there is no one else with his sales patter. Ok he is generally not that popular but give credit where it is due. The real question is: do you believe him?

There is often a Satan in many companies. They are the ones who tempt you with promises of advancement to get you to behave in a particular way. The promised rewards never materialize, often because the Satan figure does not have the power to make good their assurances. We are easily duped since we are too desperate for advancement. Beware the bearer of gifts. You will frequently find the promises will be repeated and their efficacy should wither with each recurrence.

Case Study:  Level Career Path, High Level

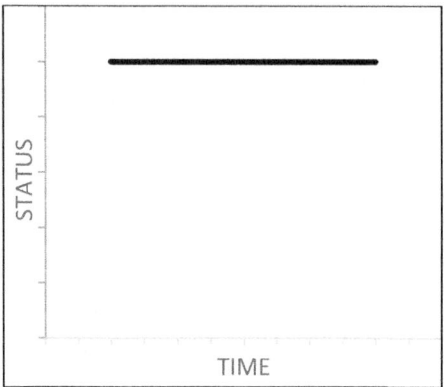

Level Career Path, High Level

Father Christmas (aka Santa Claus) is beloved by all, especially children. They, when young, believe that Father Christmas exists until their elder sibling or friend takes a malicious delight in throwing aspersions on his reality and reputed modus operandi.

Until then he is seen as the provider of requested goodies to all children who have been good across the world on one special night called Christmas Eve. These nocturnal visits involve travelling by a magic, but old fashioned, method of transport involving sleighs pulled by reindeer who have a high Status (Skills, Esteem) pulling-wise at that time of the year.

Other peculiarities are insisting on entering houses through chimneys, possibly thinking that that is the tradesman's entrance. He also consumes considerable amounts of a special type of cake and beverage kindly supplied by the parents as a reward for his generosity and labour.

As I understand it, the presents proffered on this special night have been manufactured by elves throughout the previous year. I have no idea if the elves' hierarchy have levels such as Foremen elves or

Supply Management elves (I expect they do since all companies have Supply Managers) or even if the elves are unionized. I'll get back to you on that.

Father Christmas is easily recognized by his red gown trimmed with white fur and a large white beard, which sometimes seems to move independently of his face. He is best seen prior to Christmas Eve in department stores where he will give the child a little taster of what is to come provided that the child sits on Father Christmas's knee and has their photograph taken to remember when they "believed." Children often suspect the famed aptitudes of this Father Christmas but, wisely, keep their suspicions to themselves whilst presents are forthcoming. They would wish for more than one Christmas Eve in a year but recognize that elves can only do so much.

Commentary  Father Christmas is a  good example of a high level Career Path with high level Skills with **Skills Churn** where, in this case, a generation's perspective of someone's Skills declines (in this instance, rapidly) to be replaced by a new generation with a much lower belief threshold who reinvent the high perspective. This is not uncommon with popular entertainers. Through this method he maintains an outstanding reputation even though he appears to work only day a year.

In our lives, after childhood, we probably will retain affection for one or more "magical" idols, possibly for an old teacher. They continue to give us comfort even without an annual present list. We should reflect on why it is that they were or are special and why they demonstrated such high Skills from our perspective. In reverse, we often forget that we may be that special to others: we remember that one teacher but it is probable that teacher has forgotten us. Again, a pause for reflection will do us good.

## 3.7  Class Three: Declining Career Paths

Now, finally, we consider the last our three classes of Declining Career Paths.

Case Study :  Declining Skills Low Level

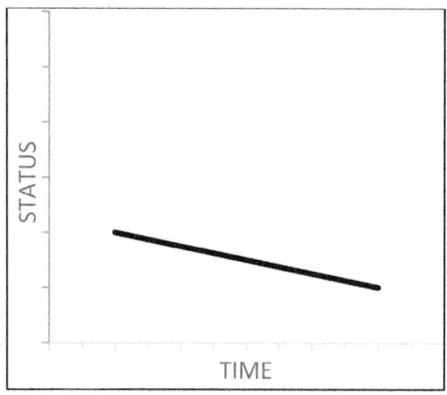

Declining Career Path, Low Level

Vincent Van Gogh was a figurative painter (though in my opinion his figures were a bit rough and ready) who lived in Holland but then moved to the South of France, a bad move since rent and painting materials were more expensive there and this led to a significant deficit in his finances. Over his time in France his Skills did not improve appreciatively and only his mate Paul and his brother Theo thought he was any good. He was quite prickly and not confident with women.

Consequently, his self-assurance declined and money ran out and even the locals laughed at him, which is something in France. He also became depressed because he had a terrible persistent earache and nobody seemed able to pronounce his name properly. He also drank a lot of absinthe with consequent effect on his painting perspective. He began to repeat himself painting vases of flowers over and over again. Vincent ended his career himself by the often-used method of suicide, supposedly in a cornfield, which was meant to be symbolic but I think that this was where he happened to be when he had finished his lunch. How he got the money for the gun is still a mystery. The ending of his life expectancy turned out to be premature because his postmortem fame rocketed when Kirk Douglas got to play him in a film.

Commentary    Vincent started out with poor Skills and it went downhill from there – a Low Level Declining Skills and Career Path. Again, however, opinions as to the progress of his Skills differ markedly depending, really, if one of your ancestors got hold of one of his paintings before his time ran out, but the perspective shown here is that of his contemporaries (excluding Theo.) Since then, of course, the perception of his Skills has blossomed but this was outside of the timeframe of his Career.

Vincent was not best served by his friend Paul and you should be suspicious of colleagues who behave as best buddies at work. We naturally bond with like-minded people but such acquaintances may not be in your best interests. Firstly, you may encourage each other in the wrong direction and secondly **Every** co-worker is a rival. Just ask yourself why it is that your excellent pal wants to be your chum. Do not go drinking at lunchtime or after work (like Vincent and Paul). It will be noticed. Sorry.Case Study:  Declining Skills Path, Medium Level

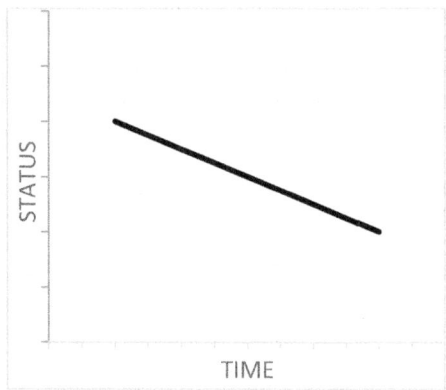

Declining Career Path, Medium Level

The Schmidts are a German dynasty and our concern with them stems from the mid seventeenth century to the mid -1950s. They are and were a house of workers in steel, specializing in fine pattern marking. In their early days they were looking around for things to fabricate (German cars had not been invented then) and hit on the idea of manufacturing the first slide rules (aka slipsticks) - two bits of metal scratched with logarithmic scales which could be rubbed together to do multiplication and division for you. Although this was a great advance and saved lots of paper covered in longhand calculations, slide rules suffered from three problems: firstly to get anything like accuracy the two bits of metal had to be about two meters long, making it hard to fit into your pocket, secondly the device did not do adding up or taking away so that you needed an abacus as well and then two devices littered your desk, and lastly you had to guess where the decimal point came in your answer, mistakes in which led to some very embarrassing engineering. They were also useless at measuring things unlike a proper ruler and not very good for drawing straight lines.

The Schmidts' slide rules, however were a great success and, as the business passed from father to son over the decades they fully deserved their reputation. But then they made their big mistake: they somehow got hold of a very advanced copy of a twentieth century marketing textbook which encouraged them to ask the question "What business are we in?" Despite their very long expertise in metal etching, they chose to become the slide rule manufacturer du jour.

So they shifted their factory in 1921 to making their slide rules out of plastic and thus faced big competition from companies whose specialty was manufacturing things out of plastic. Trade sank at an alarming rate but this was nothing compared to the tragedy in the 1970s: the invention of the electronic calculator. Now everyone of sufficient means could have a device that did all arithmetic functions on one thingy and could, moreover, help you cheat in mathematics exams. It could, even, put in the decimal point for you and work to a silly number of decimal places leading to statisticians quoting numbers to spurious levels of detail (like saying that the population of Moscow is 14,653,859.5 when all you wanted to know was whether it was bigger than London). Now slide rules were only used by that section of the populace who could not get hold of batteries. For interest, the pocket calculator was, in turn, superseded by the computer which, while at first much less portable that the calculator, could also work in Imperial weights and measures.

The Schmidts' dynasty is not what it was.

Commentary This example is chosen to illustrate that the time dimension of Career plots need not necessarily cover just a working life. The Schmidts' key Skills declined in their **applicability** over the centuries. The decline in their Career Path shows the fall in their applicable Skills even though those Skills remained in their application to metal work.

There is a chance that you work in a family business; make sure that your first interest is the business and not the family. Easy for me to say but, in such circumstances, I would leave and strike out on my own. You may have trouble finding a good excuse that does not offend your relations – perhaps easiest is to claim that you want to go out into the big wide world to gain experience there before you return to the fold. That excuse may well turn out to be the truth.

Case Study:  Declining Career Path, High Level

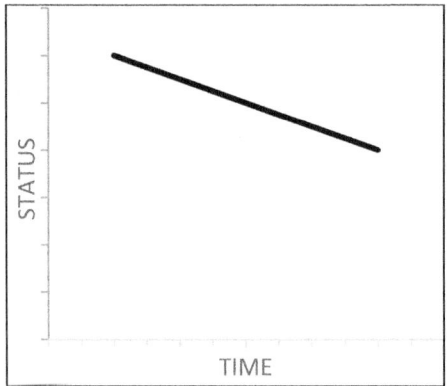

Declining Career Path, High Level

We are back with Henry 8 and this time for himself. Henry was everything a prince could be: handsome, cultured and adept, especially at the day's go-to sports of hunting obliging animals and jousting (a bit like one-on-one skittles on horseback where the skittle fights back unless it is against the king).

Henry's fatal flaw was his insistence on siring a son (bastards would not do). Despite his many attempts in this endeavor and going through six wives at the most modest reckoning, he failed. This wife-getting (and disposing thereof – in those days and in this society you could only have one wife at a time) involved many stratagems, the most momentous was declaring himself Head of the Church of England, not a popular move with the Pope who thought that he was. Monies he saved on Papal rents and rates he squandered on his wives and gambling with Thomas Cromwell (qv) so English taxes went up, not down. I guess that we are all familiar with that.

You would have thought that it would have been easier to declare himself head of another religion which allowed more than one wife so his education was maybe not that special.

Over the years of his reign Henry become increasingly grumpy: dissipated, big headed and fat. His sport changed to denouncing anybody by shouting "Ya boo traitor" and then having their heads chopped off after a little bit of torture.

Henry died a lot less admired than when he started.

Commentary  Henry starts off with High Skills, essentially due to his birth. He also presented himself well. During his reign the Skills deteriorated as he got more and more sulky. At the end of the day he was still King and you would not want to argue with that unless you fancied a bit of racking before your drawing and quartering.

For you, the dangers of being obsessed with just one aspect of your vocation will be as damaging to you as Henry's thing about fathering a son to succeed him. His mania strikes us now as ridiculous, but it was not for him. His starring role in royalty and the pressures that the affairs of State and Religion put upon him made him so.

Your passion for extraneous fragments of your business will not only seem perverse in the future but look crazy to your team mates now. You will deny that this applies to you, but I am talking about small idiosyncrasies that you will be known for, not far-reaching ambitions. Discover them and change them.

## 3.8  Perspectives on Careers

Just as perspectives on the Status of individuals vary, so do they vary on Career Paths, since these also, as we have seen, represent Skills drafted against time.

Thus from the above Career Case Studies:

- I'd wager the monks thrown out of the dissolved monasteries did not form a Thomas Cromwell fan club.
- The peers of our Assistant Marketing Manager thought her a smart-ass who kept on quoting excerpts from a stupid book at them.
- There is a significant minority of the minority in our example country who still have not got the message.
- The Royal Society for the Protection of Animals loves all dogs. It is the owners are the problem which, in this case at least, is probably right.
- I am still waiting for a decent offer for my soul from Satan, the value of which, I suppose, declines with age.
- There are a few silly people (who do not know what they are talking about) who pretend to think that Father Christmas is not real.
- The owner of the café where Van Gogh wallowed in absinthe was happy with the cash but less content with the fights.
- The Schmidts were kicked out of the Metalworkers' Guild for moving on to plastic. I am sorry, I forgot to tell you that.
- The Pope excommunicated Henry 8
-
-
-
-

## - 3.9  Conclusions and Chapter's  Key Points

The above samples of Career Paths illustrate the range of Career types to be considered in the remainder of this book. Which Class and level are you?

**The second Stage in developing Employment Plots is the use of pictograms showing Status plotted against time**

**The third stage adds Career Paths drawn on the pictograms representing Skills**

**Three Classes of Career Paths are proposed: Inclined, Level and Declined**

**Only Inclined Career Paths show Skills growing with time**

**As Career Paths show levels of Skills, they are subject to Perspectives and Comparisons**

# CHAPTER 4 OCCUPATION TRACKS and EMPLOYMENT PLOTS

## 4.1 Introduction to Occupation Tracks

The final stage in putting together my Employment Plots is the concept of **Occupation Tracks.** These are contours that are drawn on our Status/Time pictogram in the same form as Career Paths. To distinguish the two the Occupation Tracks are dotted as in the model below:

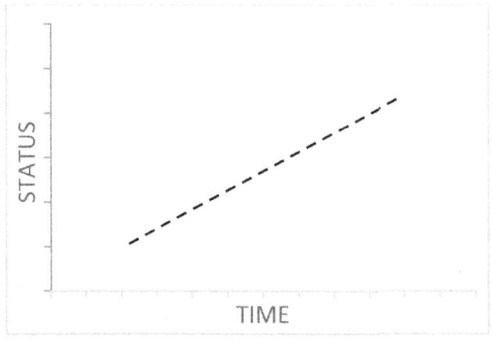

Model Occupation Track

Occupation Tracks are representations of developing work levels, for example:

Dispenser to Chief Pharmacist

Tennis Rookie to Major Winner

Local Counsellor to Prime Minister

Charity Fundraiser to Charity CEO

Again, these Tracks, as with all else in Employment Plots, are symbols for real occupations and are models, not actual jobs. Occupation Tracks are the draft of positions that are offered in an Organisation that are **possible** e.g. "Finance Assistant" rising to "Finance Director". These positions do not actually have to be held by someone.

This should be compared with Career Paths which represent the possible progress of an actual person. The important difference between Career Paths and Occupation Tracks is that Career Paths draw **Skills** against time, and Occupations Tracks draw **Wealth & Esteem against the same time.** Both, of course, are elements of Status, although as we are comparing apples with pears at least they are grown in the same orchard.

## 4.2  Extent of Occupation Tracks

### Case Study:  The Big Top

Maisie, a young and impressionable girl, falls in love with a slightly older youth who works as the front end of a pantomime horse in a travelling circus. She soon joins him as the back end as well as sharing his caravan; despite my extensive research I found no information as to what happened to the erstwhile rear end.

Just like the age-old story, love does not last and Maisie is turfed out of the caravan and the vocation. The circus owner is fond of her and keeps her on as the rope holder for the acrobatic team. Maisie is a quick learner and soon climbs the ranks of the squad, but gets bored with the repetitive exercises and lack of thrills and danger (Health and Safety unreasonably required a safety net.)

She moves onwards and upwards to train as a lion tamer. In due course, her principal and instructor retire and Maisie takes over. "Pity the poor pupil who does not surpass his master" (Leonardo, believe it or not). Her specialty is putting her head into the lion's mouth. I have not heard of her for some time now - perhaps she has retired?

Commentary How do we draft Maisie's Occupation Track(s)? At first sight we need three Tracks: one for her rear end, one for her gymnastics and one for her feline exertions. My proposition is that she needs but one – that of circus entertainer. Occupation Tracks need to reflect the broad employment possibilities. If you hear echoes of marketing's "What business are we in" then your aural sensitivities are precise.

However, should Maisie have significantly changed her career from the circus to that of, say, fighter jet pilot or betting shop clerk, then we would need to draft new Organisation Plots (see 4.10 Double (and Multiple) Vectors below).

## 4.3 Different Occupations within Organisations

Organisations (please note capital "O") here are enterprises that offer employment to workers. Some Organisations will be small and only offer one Occupation Track; other will be larger and able to offer more than one:

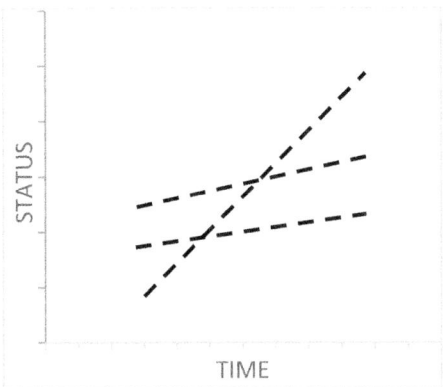

Different Occupation Tracks offered by an Organisation

Here we can see three different Occupation Tracks shown on one Employment Plot; they could, for instance, illustrate jobs in finance, transport or secretarial sectors.

## 4.4 Classes of Occupation Tracks

Just as with Career Paths, I propose three Classes of Occupation Tracks:

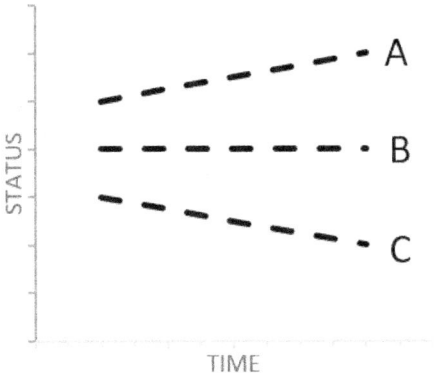

Classes of Occupation Tracks

The above plot represents the three classes of model Occupation Tracks. Just as with Careers, Wealth & Esteem can incline with time (A), be Level with time (B) and decline with time (C). Status can be plotted because Organisations offer levels of Wealth and Esteem to their employees.

Model A (Inclining) is the hierarchical model with possible Wealth & Esteem rising with time. This is the class that pictures companies (in the broadest sense) offering vocational progress. Over time, the Office Junior can rise up the Occupation Track until he or she reaches Managing Director (in theory, at least and unlikely in practice). This Class of Occupations is **hierarchical** with stages going up a "ladder" to which employees aspire.

Model B (level) is non-hierarchical with no rising of Wealth & Esteem with time. Many occupations are like this: there is only one level on offer by the organization, for instance "Bus Driver"; although the bus company will have lower and higher jobs (such as cleaner or timetable manager) the position of Driver is usually the only one available to a large group of employees.

Model C (Declining) is the reverse of Model A and shows declining Wealth & Esteem with Time and thus hierarchical in decay: the longer you stay in that occupation the lower will be your rewards.

As examples, the Plot above could represent Occupation Tracks for A= Sales & marketing where there are levels that increase with time, B= Assembly Line worker where there is no opportunity for promotion, and C= drivers who are made redundant.

## 4.5 At Last! Employment Plots

You can overlay a Career Path and an Occupation Track together on our Status/Time pictogram to form an **Employment Plot,** provided that they cover the same time period. At any point in time the Status levels of the Career (Skills) and Occupation (Wealth and Esteem) can be **compared:**

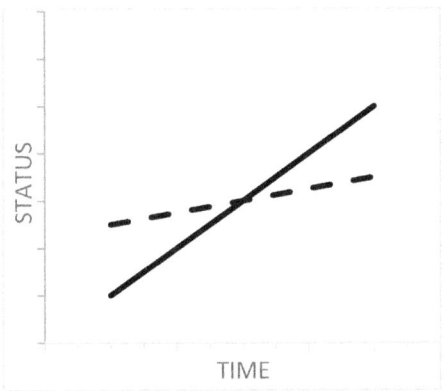

Model Employment Plot

So in the Model Employment Plot above:

**The chart itself denotes an Organisation**

**The Occupation Track (dotted line) denotes the Wealth & Esteem levels for a particular role in the Organisation**

**The Career Path (solid line) denotes Skills utilized in the Organisation by an Individual**

Employment Plots are intended to show, for an employee, the relative Status levels between his or her Skills in an organization (at a point in time on his Career Path) and the Wealth & Esteem level of the position held on the Occupation Track. In this model we have an Inclining Career Path drawn with an Inclining Occupation Track; the idea is that we can, through the time period of the plot, compare the actual Skills of the individual vertically (i.e. at any one time) on the

Career Path with the possible Wealth & Esteem provided by the Occupation Track.

At any point in time of the Plot the employee is offering his or her Skills in exchange for Wealth and Esteem and the organization is offering Wealth and Esteem in exchange for the employee's Skills.

**The Careers of individuals provide Skills in Exchange for Wealth and Esteem**

**Organisations provide Wealth and Esteem for the Skills of that individual as represented by Occupation Tracks**

Large Organisations will offer several Occupation Tracks expressing different roles e.g. Sales, Marketing, Finance, HR etc. The Employment Plot as a whole is intended to represent the Organisation, which can be made up of several possible Occupations and, probably, several individuals' Careers. The careers can be drawn as Career Paths and then compared with the corresponding Occupation Tracks.

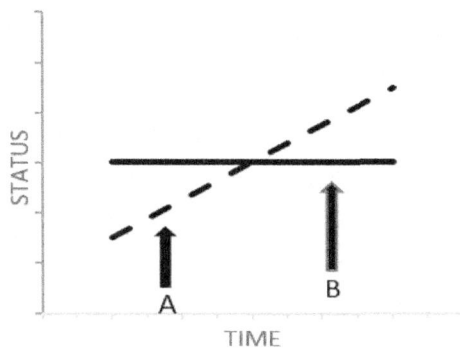

Employment Plot Showing Two Points in Time

Therefore, in this Employment Plot above, at point A in time the Career Path (solid line) is above the Occupation Track (dotted line): the individual's Status is higher because their Skills are above what are required in their job and the Wealth and Esteem provided by the Occupation are below what the employee deserves. The individual is **Under Regarded** or, to follow Dr. Peter's designation, he or she is **Competent**. Similarly, when our individual reaches point B in time they are now **Over Regarded** having lower Skills than required by their Occupation. These employees are designated **Incompetent** by Dr. Peter. Competence and Incompetence are key concepts in Dr. Peter's work (and the same here.)

## 4.6  Time Period of Employment Plots

The timeframe for Employment Plots is that point where an individual's Career Path and Occupation Track **coincide in time**. That might be a whole working life or it might be very short e.g. my career as lead guitarist in my student rock band. (Where oh where did it all go wrong?)

## 4.7 Natural Justice and the Ratchet Effect

You may think that a person's Skills offered to an Organisation, and the Wealth and Esteem that he or she receives in return, should have a natural balance. Excess Skills should, in due time, merit greater rewards. Similarly, not being up to a job should result in demotion.

This idea comes from a sense of natural justice together with, in capitalist societies, the working of market forces.

This is, however, not necessarily the case.

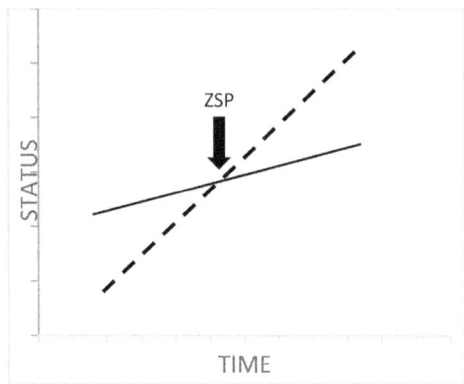

Model Employment Plot Showing ZSP

In the above figure I have designated the point where Skills on the Career Path match the Wealth & Esteem on the Occupation Track the **Zero Sum Point (ZSP).** The simple fact is that employees can and do move up their Path beyond their ZSP and get promoted, to a point where their received Wealth & Esteem is greater than their provided Skills. You will have noticed the similarity between my ZSPs and Dr. Peter's point when an employee is promoted to their level of Incompetence. We will be considering this in Chapter 10.

There is no absolute perspective of Status. You (obviously) are under-regarded but, for your staff, you are clearly over-regarded. None of you are "right". The best way to determine where you are on your Career Path is to ask yourself whether you are frustrated in your work or slightly embarrassed.

What about moving back down your Career Path? This is a good place to introduce the **Ratchet Effect.** An **Inclined** Career Path on an Employment plot is not a game of Snakes and Ladders — you can, basically, only go upwards. As our individual moves forward in time he or she cannot move down the Career Path because of its positive Inclination. Only very rarely will someone be demoted; the usual method to rebalance deficits in Skills versus remuneration (which includes Esteem) is to fire the undeserving thief.

Of course, individuals can and do take career breaks which may result in a loss of Skills and therefore a drop down their Career Path.

## 4.8  Examples of Employment Plots

If there are three Classes of Occupation Tracks at three levels, and the same for Career Paths, then your computer will tell you there are eighty one possible combinations (80.999999 if you used a calculator). You will be relieved to hear that we will not consider all of them, but rather concentrate our attention on those permutations that are the most illuminating. To get you used to Employment plots we can re-examine the nine Career Paths from Chapter 3 with their equivalent Occupation Tracks forming Employment Plots.

In particular you should note the flexibility and broad application of Employment plots to the scenarios chosen for this purpose. Please remember that Employment Plots show **actual** Career levels against **possible** Occupation levels in the Organisation.

Case Study:  Thomas Cromwell Redux

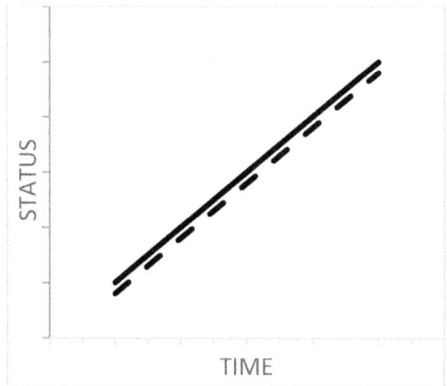

Employment Plot for Thomas Cromwell

Commentary  The Organisation plotted is Merry England; Thomas's occupation is that of a general factotum, a "fixer". That occupation, as provided by sixteenth century England, went from the very low to the very high. Thomas rode that incline all the way up from blacksmith's assistant to the King's Master Secretary. Note that he achieved this by always having a Career Path above the Occupation Track which encouraged promotion.

We should learn from history: fixing our future on one seemingly powerful man or woman as Thomas did twice can lead to rapid progress. Unfortunately, that star in your company firmament may lose their position or say goodbye to that business leaving you stranded. Better that, though, than having your head chopped off.

Case Study:   Assistant Marketing Manager Redux

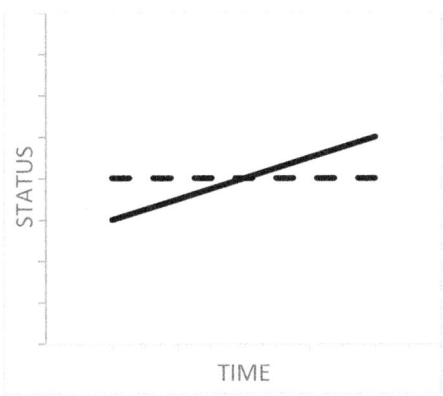

<u>Employment Plot for the Assistant Marketing Manager</u>

<u>Commentary</u>  The Organisation plotted is the company in which our Assistant Marketing Manager toils. Her occupation is a common one. Her Career starts with inadequate Skills compared with those required by her firm, but as she is promoted due to her outstanding knowledge provided by a certain book, her Skills rise higher than her lowly company can provide in terms of Wealth and Esteem (i.e. Status). She should resign and move to a company that will recognize her talents. She moves from Incompetent to Competent.

The existence of a continuous and extensive Occupation Track as provided by an employer does not, in itself, guarantee progress along it. If you make extra efforts outside of the workplace to improve your Skills then it is unlikely that they will be recognized. Time to move on to where they are.

Case Study: Nelson Mandela Redux

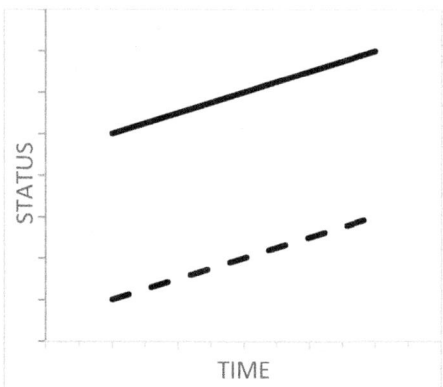

Employment Plot for Nelson Mandela

Commentary The Organisation plotted is that unequal society. Nelson's Occupation Track reflects his opportunities work-wise as part of the majority population for all of his life. In fact they are higher than most of his fellows, his training as a lawyer means he was not at rock bottom. His career consistently outperforms the Occupation offered to the Organisation (i.e. the State). What the Employment Plot demonstrates in how far the lines are apart is how much his Career Skills massively outweigh his rewards. The condition of Competence personified.

We are all not as saintly as Nelson. The lack of recognition of our Skills in our Organisation (reflected in inadequate Wealth and Esteem) can be so frustrating that Self Esteem is damaged. As with Nelson, try to be patient (though hopefully not for twenty years).

Occupation Tracks can often be invisible and you never know what is just around the corner. As he discovered.

## Case Study:  The Dog Redux

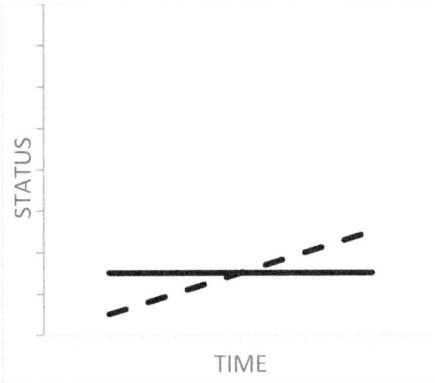

Employment Plot for the Dog

Commentary The Organisation plotted is the two joint households. Even Mrs. Gently accepts that the dog had charms as a puppy which, at that time, were deemed superior to his naughty sanitary habits (Career Path above Occupation Track) but this Esteem soon disappears as he matures. Occupation-wise, dogs are supposed to develop from badly behaved puppies to old and trusty companions, which is why we mourn them when they are called to that great kennel in the sky. Their Occupation Track rises with Time. Not much is asked of this particular dog but, from Mrs.Gently's perspective, he is a constant and persistent pain and does not follow the usual doggie progress.

The dog's role in life is pretty small as is the case that for many people. Having a "menial" job is no bar to trying to do your best. Although Skills are presumably low, not too much is asked of our dog. We all know persons who perform "lowly" jobs with admirable dedication and industry and, quite rightly, we Esteem them. Do not be a bad dog – shake-a-paw nicely and go to your basket when told.

Case Study:  Satan Redux

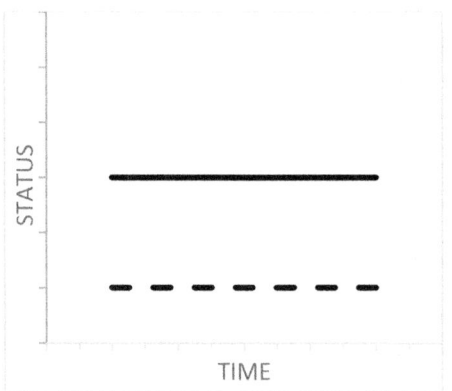

Employment Plot for Satan

Commentary Please note that the time period for this Case Study is eternity. The Organisation plotted is the Universe. Satan's Occupation Track does not change much throughout his "lifetime" and there is no prospect of career advancement. He may aspire to replacing God but that opportunity is not on offer by the sphere in which they operate. Satan's employment gives good Wealth (assuming the exchange rate for souls is OK currently) but offers little Esteem amongst the general population. However good or bad you think his role in life is, you have to admit that he is very good at it. Notice that there is only one Satan and thus he is not in a hierarchy, which is why he probably left the gang of Angels in a sulk as he was not top dog. Always Competent.

We can often get stuck in our profession, just like Satan, with about as much chance of improvement. We have, basically, two choices: move to another pursuit and new Organisation and Occupation Track or stay where we are and increase our apparent Skills via other means (job on the side? Marry the boss's daughter? Embezzlement?)

Case Study: Father Christmas Redux

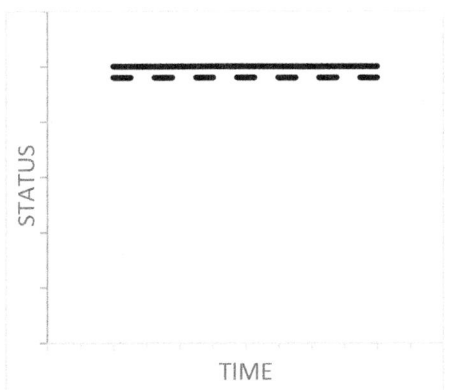

Employment Plot for Father Christmas

Commentary N.B. When the Career Paths and Occupation Tracks are drawn together they are meant to be at the same Status level. Quirk of the Plots. You could, if you were so **inclined** (joke), draw three dimensional plots for a whole organization showing multiple Occupation Tracks and Career Paths. Further research and a Super Computer to handle it depends on **further funding, please.**

For Father Christmas the very high levels of Skills demanded by his Occupation are met across his (hopefully) long life. His Occupation (like Satan's) does not offer opportunities for advancement and the Track is consequently flat.

He, and his occupation, are one of a select band of mythical figures extant in other cultures and religions whose appearance and actions are similar to his so, I suppose, that with his Skills he could switch and maintain his Status. I am presuming that Saint Nicholas and others operate at the same occupational level and I could be wrong (but only in this insignificant point, you understand).

For this special person we can take a special view of the time period of this Employment Plot; let us assume that it is one year. Father Christmas seems to do his main job in 24 hours in the whole of that year. There is part time and there is part time!

In actuality, unless we work 24 hours a day we all work part time, it is just a question of how much. One of the curses of modern life is that the seeking of Work Status has overwhelmed that of Life Status. You will not receive extra Wealth and Esteem by working longer hours than you are paid for, believe it or not.

One likely aspect of this curse is receiving, and being expected to respond to, emails, 'phone calls and texts outside of "office hours." My recommendations are these: firstly, never ever respond to emails in your own time. Even better, never read them. Your boss and colleagues will soon understand that you will not read them or reply and give up. Secondly, if you answer a 'phone call or text, always wait a couple of hours and then ring or text them back with a question, answer, comment or whatever. The later the better. Only by doing this persistently will your caller begin to understand how irritating these calls are.

Case Study:  Van Gogh Redux

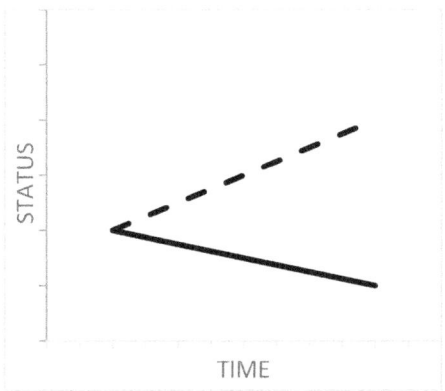

Employment Plot for Van Gogh

Commentary   The Organisation plotted is the artist's world; the Occupation Track for Vincent symbolizes nineteenth century painters. Note that if it represented sixteenth century painters it would be a longer and steeper line because they could achieve higher Esteem than their Impressionist disciples.

The timeframe is Vincent's painting life (i.e. Career) since the Occupation Track does not offer a position to dead artists. Hence what happened to the appreciation of his Skills after his demise is not covered by the Employment Plot.

He is a good example of "flogging a dead horse" graft-wise. Many of us aim to be successful in vocations in which we do not have, or cannot develop, sufficient Skills. Rather than change course we can persist, against all odds, with endeavours in which we cannot win. This is especially the case where desired callings have very high Wealth and Esteem. Too many girls want to be models, too many boys want to be best-selling authors of management books (or footballers if they wrongly think that sporting Esteem could possibly be higher than that of literary geniuses.)

Case Study:  The Schmidts Redux

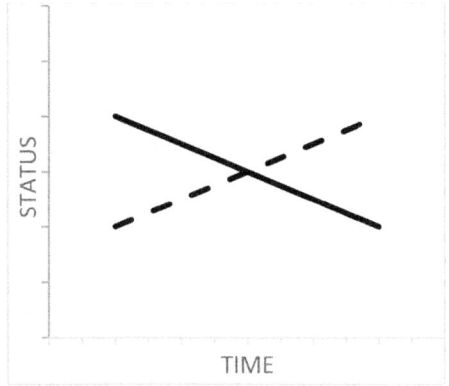

Employment Plot for the Schmidts

Commentary   The Organisation is the calculating domain. What business are the Schmidts in? This Occupation Track represents "Slide Rule Manufacturing" rather than "Steel Fabricators" which could show a different Occupation Track and thus a different Employment Plot. Because of this choice of theirs, the Career Path declines as they do not have any comparative Skills.

Choosing the wrong occupation, especially at the beginning of a career, can make or break your Status. Of course, it is often difficult to make that choice, particularly since to pursue many professions you have to resolve to do so and commit to them early in life. Once you choose to be a Doctor or piano teacher you really are stuck with it.

Your Career is inextricably hooked onto Occupation Tracks; you can change the Organisation who will offer a different Occupation Track, but check that you can meet the Skills required in that new Occupation. Moving from Competent to Incompetent is worse than "frying pan to fire".

Case Study:  Henry 8 Redux

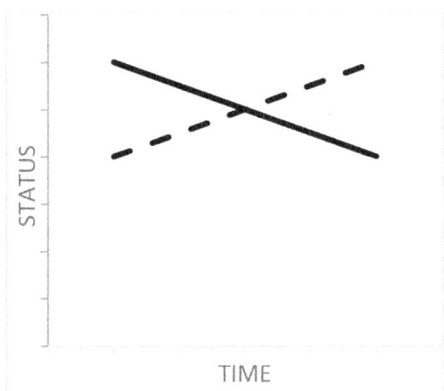

Employment Plot for Henry 8

Commentary___Henry's Occupation Line is "Kingship". What is expected of a King is that, as he matures through his reign, his Skills increase with experience. Unfortunately Henry's sovereignty goes in the opposite direction and he moves from a competent monarch to an incompetent despot.

I have some sympathy with him. When we look up to the CEO of our company we are envious of their position and guess that their job is much like yours or mine but better rewarded. We do not imagine that there is a special strain on such a role: loneliness. You have your colleagues, staff and manager support; she is (a) on her own and (b) her mistakes cannot be rectified by anyone above her. Perhaps enough to turn anyone into a tyrant. She must be careful of any personal relationship, cannot go to the pub with you and "the buck stops there". You would be surprised how many CEOs or equivalent would seriously consider dropping down the company thereby increasing Life Status whilst reducing Work Status. When you hear of executives "Stepping Down" you may take a good guess at why.

## 4.9 Vertical Occupation Tracks

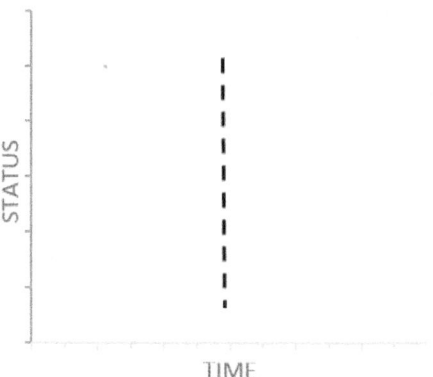

Vertical Occupation Track

For the sake of completeness there is another Occupation Track presented for your consideration. This shape can only occur for a very brief moment as it stands on a single twinkling in time. There is no before or after. It can happen in very rare circumstances and is a much sought after collectors' item.

# 4.10 Double (and Multiple) Vectors

It is perfectly possible (and often instructive) to draft two Career Paths (or more) or two Occupation Tracks (or more) on the same Employment Plot:

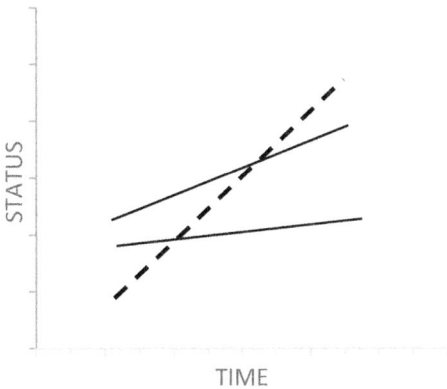

Employment Plot with Two Career Paths, One Occupation Track

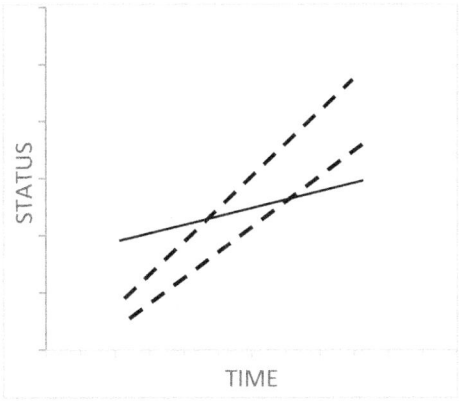

Employment Plot with Two Occupation Tracks, One Career Path

In the two models above we can use the Employment Plots to compare two Careers (perhaps you and a competitor?) or compare two different Occupations that may be available to you.

Of course you are not limited to just two; you can draft as many Paths or Tracks as you need, but I do not recommend combining more than one Career Path **and** more than one Occupation Track on the same Plot. Employment Plots are meant to be simple visual expressions of employment scenarios, not Jackson Pollock sketches. When you draft double or multiple Plots you must be careful to ensure that all Career Paths and Occupation Tracks cover **the same time period**.

We will be using these "multiple" Plots throughout the rest of the book.

## 4.11 Conclusions and Chapter's Key Points

I trust that you are now sufficiently confident with the idea of Employment Plots. We can now move forward to examine a large variety of Organisations, together with their Occupation Tracks, and the comparisons of Careers via the medium of these devices. One thing needs emphasizing again: these plots are **models** which describe what can **possibly** happen and not what actually does or could. How far you claw your way up the Career path is up to you. Higher Career Skills will lead to higher Wealth and Esteem. We will analyse several different examples of Employment Plots; hopefully you will use these Plots to reflect on your career and those of your competitors.

Employment Plots represent Organisations

Different Occupations within those Organisations are represented by Occupation Tracks drawn on the Plots showing the Wealth and Esteem parts of Status

Individual Careers are represented by lines drawn on the Plots showing the Skills part of Status

Occupation Tracks belong to the same three classes as Career Paths: Inclined, Level and Declined

On the Plots, an Individual's Skills can be compared to their Occupation's Wealth & Esteem at any point in time.

For an individual, Skills tend to balance Wealth & Esteem in an Organisation including the one you work in!

# CHAPTER 5  REGULAR INCLINED OCCUPATION TRACKS

## 5.1. Introduction

The three Classes of Occupation Tracks described in the previous chapter are what I call **Regular**: they, together with Career Paths, are represented by straight lines.

Chapters 5, 6 and 7 will each consider these three classes of regular Occupation Tracks (Inclined, Level, Declined) and the Organisations that provide them.

This chapter covers **Inclined** Occupation Tracks **only**. Remember that they are drawn with dotted lines. All classes of Career Paths (solid lines) are illustrated below with suitable Case Studies: dotted = Occupation Tracks, solid = Career Paths.

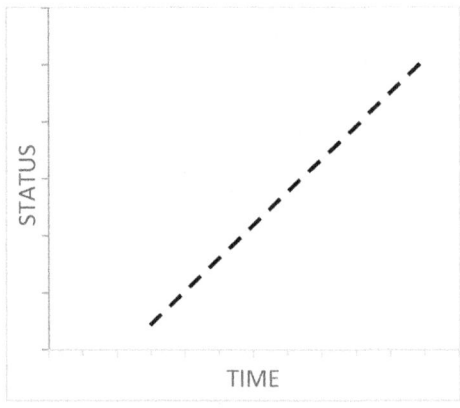

Model of Inclining Occupation Track

Since this class of Occupation Track is the most common in any organisation involving management grades - which is therefore hierarchical - I give it the most attention. In order to, perhaps, simplify things I have chosen all my Case Studies in this chapter from one such Organisation, "Happy Hospital".

## 5.2  Inclined Career Paths : Crossing

Once again, since this will be the model Employment Plot of most interest to budding managers (who might reasonably expect to increase their Skills over their working lives) this section is the most detailed. In this model both the Occupation Track and the Career Path are Inclined and, in addition, they **cross**.

Case Study:  Only So Far

As an example, we choose a Bright Lad whose Career Path rises from his beginnings as an Administrative Assistant and then has the potential, at least, to rise through the ranks of Junior Administrator though Administrator, Senior Administrator, Administration Manager, Senior Administrative Manager, Deputy Administration Director onto the glorious peak of Administration Director. Unfortunately, Bright Lad is only a little luminous and the reality is that he will only go a little way up the ladder.  So, our first and most important Employment plot is:

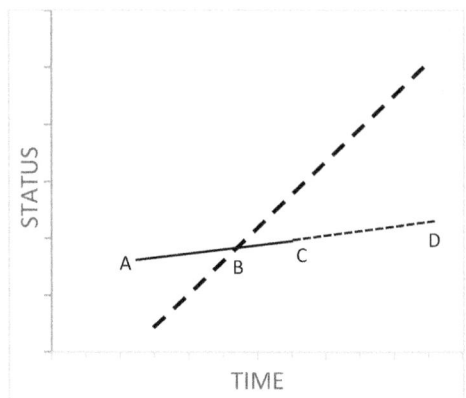

Possible Employment Plots for Bright Lad

Commentary   Bright Lad's Occupation Track goes, over the timeframe of his Career Path, from Junior Administrator to Administration Director. Realistically, however, he would be delighted to end his Career at a much lower rank.

His starts as a Junior Administrator at point A. At this level his Skill outweighs his received Wealth and Esteem; that injustice is corrected and more as he increases his Skills to point B, when he is promoted to the position of Administrator. At this point, his ZSP, his Skills and received Wealth & Esteem are, as they morally and commercially should be, in balance. **In most real-life circumstances this is how things remain.** We rise up the company until our rewards fairly reflect our talents. But it ain't necessarily so!

Finding Administration staff at Happy Hospital is proving difficult; the HR department is, quite frankly, not the best in the world. A vacancy arises for a Senior Administrator and Bright Lad and his rival Administrator, Dim but Warm, are the only two internal applicants. The HR department has failed to get an advertisement inviting external applications for the post out in time so, when the time comes for interviews and selection, only the two internal candidates present themselves. Some on the interviewing panel are all for delaying the election, but the HR manager, to cover herself, pretends that they have not obtained any external applications.

By force majeur the panel is obliged to choose Bright Lad and he is promoted. Happy Lad indeed!

Further Commentary Now at point C on the Employment Plot, Happy Lad's Skills do not justify the Wealth and Esteem that go with his new role. Most of the Administration staff mildly resent this, but accept it because (1) Bright Lad is actually quite nice, (2) he is not, by any means, the worst example of over-promotion at Happy Hospital and (3) their chance of the same type of elevation might happen and they can quote the upgrading of Bright Lad as a fortunate precedent.

Note that Bright Lad, although he can see an Occupation Track stretching ever onwards and upwards, does not dream of further advancement along it and never expects to progress to point D, his Career ends at point C on his retirement.

In theory we could have an Inclined/Inclined Employment Plot with the Career Path reversed with the Occupation Track:

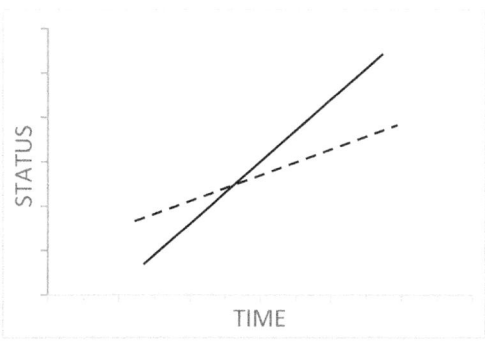

Employment Plot with Steeper Career Path than Occupation Track

Possible yes, but very unlikely as (a) the individual is not going to achieve higher Wealth & Esteem than his Skills in the early part of his working life and (b) is not going to accept much lower rewards than his talents deserve in the future.

## 5.3 Inclined Career Paths: Not Crossing (Skills>Wealth/Esteem)

In this next model the Skills of our individual are **always** greater than the rewards of Wealth and Esteem. The Career Path and the Occupation Track do not cross.

Case Study:  The Angel

The scene is the occasion of the retirement party for Nurse Terrific. For once, this is not held in a side room of one of the wards. Hundreds want to come to thank Nurse Terrific for all that she has done over her entire career at Happy Hospital and a local hall has been hired. Ecstatic praise rolls in from representatives of all the grateful parties she has inspired during her time at Happy Hospital: patients whose lives she has saved, families of patients whose final days she has miraculously comforted, more junior nurses whom she has inspired and trained, fellow professionals whose work has been so wonderfully helped, Board members who have gained so much from her sagacious advice... No one can think of, let alone voice, the slightest criticism. The proverbial angel.

A collection has been made to recognize Nurse Terrific's immaculate Career, which is astounding, but only reflects on this saint who, on top of everything else, is utterly modest.

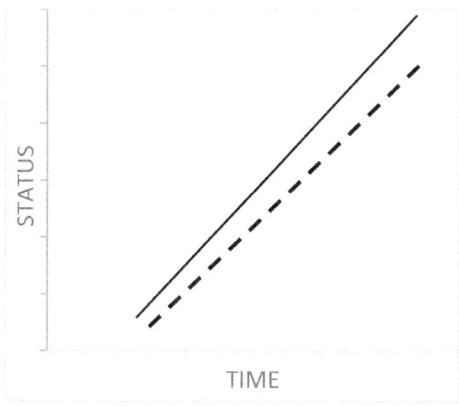

Employment Plot for Nurse Terrific

Commentary Nurse Terrific's Career Path is above her Occupation Track (Skill greater than Wealth and Esteem) throughout her Career. At first, if you are like me, then you think that the Nurse Terrifics of this world are few and far between. Part of this is driven by envy of those above us and another part reflects the simple fact that we do not understand the responsibilities of our superiors and therefore underestimate them.

I like to think now that the Nurse Terrific is the rule rather than the exception when I am taken to hospital.

# 5.4 Inclined Career Paths: Not Crossing (Skills<Wealth/Esteem)

In this model the Skills of our specimen worker are always **less** than the recompense of Wealth and Esteem. The Career Path again does not cross the Occupation Track but this time it runs below it.

Case Study: Anxiety!

The Happy Hospital specialises in Paediatric cancers; Dr. Troubled is half way through her time there, between her arrival as a Junior

Doctor and the usual date for retirement. Her position is Paediatric Consultant dedicated to children's cancers.

From all angles she is very competent. From all angles except one: everytime a child under her care does not make it she is horribly affected and blames herself no matter how diligent she has been. She thinks that she cannot face the parents of the unfortunate children feeling that she has let them down dramatically.

No amount of further training assuages this despondency, despite its acceleration of her Skills. After working half the usual time in her profession she resigns in order to reduce her stress.

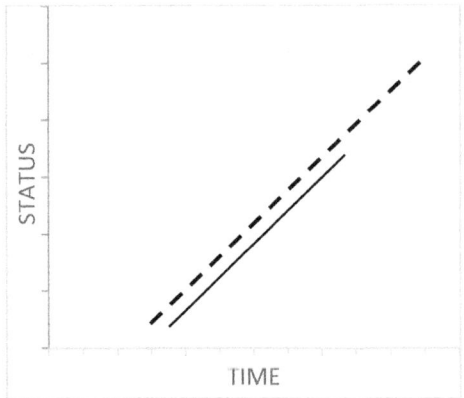

Employment Plot for Dr. Troubled

Commentary How come Dr. Troubled's Career Path (Skills) is below her Occupation Track? The answer is that it is her own perspective that I have modelled; were we to consider the perspective of her colleagues then the Plot would be a truncated version of Nurse Terrific's above. Note that Dr. Troubled feels that her inability to face parents is her only "fault", so her Career Path is just shy of the Occupation Track.

In this case it is Dr. Troubled herself who decides not to take up the possibilities of further promotion offered by a Consultant's Occupation Track.

They key issue here is that of Job Satisfaction (see 2.16 above). Her "fault" is actually affecting her Life as much as her Work Status. Work Wealth and Esteem are, of course, important to us, but sometimes the cost of succeeding in those terms is not worth the costs to our lives outside of work. Although, as I have said, my main concern in this book is Work Status, Total Status is a combination of that with Life Status. Many, many people regard their "life" to be more important than their vocation; the trick is to get the right balance in order to maximize Total Status.

## 5.5 Level Career Paths (High)

Level Career Paths show no increase in Skills over time. This, in turn, should mean no increase in corresponding Wealth and Status. Whereas Inclined Career Paths can proceed beyond the ZSP (the point where Under Regarded move to Over Regarded) Level Career Paths stop at that point. Examples are now provided of **Level Career Paths** plotted against our **Inclined Occupation Tracks** at three levels (High, Medium and Low.)

### Case Study:  The Old Boy Network

Giles, a banker, meets an old chum, Jasper, who has a senior position in the government trade department. The venue is the annual alumni University College get-together. As they sit together luxuriating with their '18 Armagnac and Cohibas they warmly reminisce about memories of their university days, most of which are wildly exaggerated.

The reveries move on to their school days (did I forgot to tell you, they went to the same school? I expect that you are not surprised). They converse:

Jasper, "Yes, Giles you were the best fag I had. Especially when you covered up for me with Matron when we got drunk and I was sick all over Justin. I look back on those days and often wonder whether I should have been more appreciative."

Giles, "Well, it's never too late, old boy."

Jasper, "You, of all people, don't want for anything, surely. That nice little sinecure at the bank must look after the necessaries."

Gils, "Well, actually, there is a tiny wee problem with the bank. Nothing serious, of course, but it looks as if I might need to keep my head down for a bit. Bit of furlough if you get my drift."

Jasper, "Oh dear, that's a terrible shame, Marion will be most upset."

Giles, "My wife doesn't know about it, nor should she. She would not understand these petty tribulations."

Jasper, "Well, I am sure that it will all die down. I am not sure how I can help. The department watches out for any sign of favouritism like a hawk".

Giles, "Of course not, Jasper. I just wondered if there was a chance that one of your colleagues in another department owes you a teeny courtesy."

Jasper, "I'll have a poke around. There's old thingy at Health who's somewhat obliged to me at the moment. To change the subject, do you remember old whatsit getting rusticated for secreting naughty substances when in fact they were mine?"

Time passes. Jasper invites Giles to lunch (on the department, naturally).

Jasper, "Nothing has come out about your slight difficulty as far as I know. Well camouflaged! This Montrachet is quite quite good, don't you think? Thingy has come up with one or two suggestions. The Chairman of the Board at Happy Hospital Group is persona non grata at the moment; apparently, he has been taking decisions off his own bat. Thingy suggests shoving him out to grass leaving a vacancy, which he thinks he could swing for you. Of course, it is nothing like as grand as your old job but any port in a storm, eh? Your pad is in the region so we can make it look local, reasonable and convenient."

Giles, "That is awfully awfully kind of you and Thingy. I will look forward to an opportunity to repay you both."

Jasper, "So will I, Giles old friend. So will I."

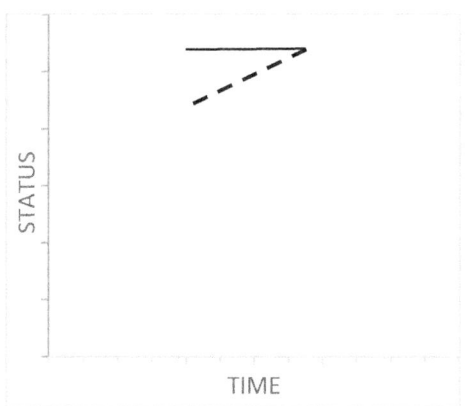

Employment Plot for the Board Chairman

Commentary This Plot shows the Organisation Track for Board members with few posts but all at a high level of Wealth and Esteem.

Giles (for his time on the Board (and for the timeframe of the Plot) goes in at the top as Chairman and stays there.

You will, of course, question why Giles' Skills are shown as so high when he is probably pretty useless at the job; the reason is that "who you know" is a substantial Skill in itself and, in this case, outweighs any "what you know" deficiencies. We all complain loudly and bitterly about people getting jobs on the basis of "who they know" but I ask you to reflect on your own career and enquire of yourself if, in perhaps just the smallest way, you took advantage of this stratagem. If you have not then it is you that is missing that Skill.

## 5.6 Level Career Paths (Medium)

Case Study: The Old Fogey

Felicity joins the Happy Hospital as a pharmacist straight from university. Felicity is happy in her job and stays in it all her life; she is not ambitious and is one of those annoying people who disdains the rat race all her fellow pharmacists are in. Accordingly, she is not popular and, to make things worse, she doesn't seem to care about it. She is never found to be not up to her occupation and is never thought of when promotion opportunities arise. Of course, she is never demoted.

She makes no efforts to improve her Skills. She does not attend extra pharmacy courses or try anything new. She can be rude to her boss and affects not to know who her boss's boss is. As she goes through her Career there is no progress in her Status; she goes from "Young Felicity" to "Felicity" and then "Old Felicity". She retires at the same level in the pharmacy stakes as when she landed.

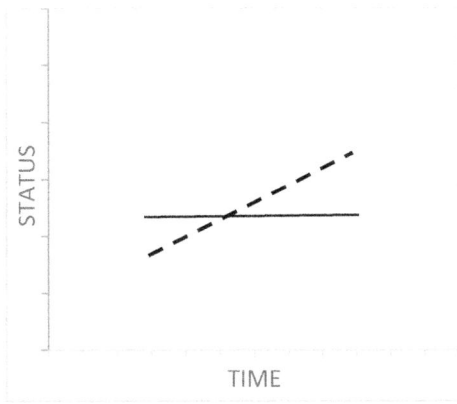

Employment Plot for the Pharmacist

Commentary Felicity is one who chooses not to partake in this game of life and she is not alone. Her Career Path starts at Happy Hospital as a newly qualified pharmacist with her Skills above her rewards. Over time, she does not improve her Skills and her Career ends at the same level as when she started. Meanwhile her Wealth and Esteem grow by the usual annual increments until she reaches the top of the scale for her position, which is the same at which she started. Note that her Career Line continues past her ZSP but she does not take the possibilities available to her.

A key concept in this book is that it is natural to want to increase your Status and that the best way to achieve this is to increase your Skills through the equivalence of Skills and Wealth & Esteem. However, ambition in the population is likely to distribute along the usual Bell Curve and Felicity will not be the only one at the lower end.

## 5.7 Level Career Paths: (Low)

### Case Study: Cleanliness is Next to Godliness

Mary is a Ward Cleaner at Happy Hospital Group. She is a single mother and works five shifts a week at the hospital and has two other part time jobs that are necessary to make ends meet. Mary is very diligent in her work as she understands how important it is to keep everything in her wards spick and span to prevent germs spreading. Often, she works unpaid overtime to make sure that things are exactly as she would want them. She is as professional as anyone there, but other staff often take her for granted, asking her to do things that are not in her job description, and she always tries to accommodate them. Mary has no ambitions to be anything other than a Ward Cleaner and, in fact, is happy to have this job.

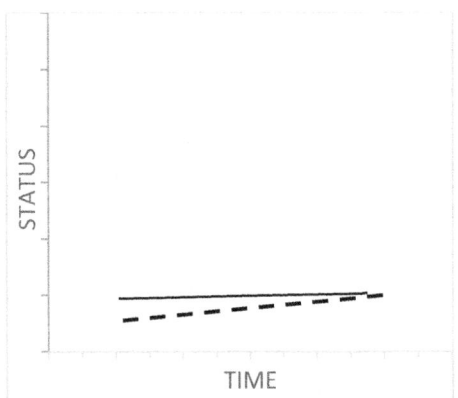

Employment Plot for the Hospital Cleaner

Mary's Occupation Track is very shallow; there are no prospects for her to develop new Skills and thus increase her Wealth and Esteem. Despite her dedication to her work and its value to Happy Hospital, her Occupation Track limits her rewards. There is no natural relationship between Skills and their "value" and thus (because of the equivalence between Skills and Wealth & Esteem) no accepted relationship between what she put into her job and what she gets out.

# 5.8  Declining Career Paths

In the above cases we have considered, relative to Inclining Occupation Tracks, Inclining Career Paths (as the most common) and Level Career Paths (The next most common).  So now we must examine, at least for the sake of completeness, the unusual instance of Declining Career Paths against Inclined Occupation Tracks. Due to the infrequent occurrence of this type of Employment Plot only one example is provided.

Case Study:  Dipsomania

Arthur is employed in the Finance Department at Happy Hospital as an Invoices Controller. As we will see, it is very fortunate that he does not have any contact with patients or, indeed, many staff. This is because Arthur is an alcoholic. His problems began before he was appointed and the Personnel Department did not follow up on his references or pick up on the hints from his previous company.

His behaviour worsens. Initially his colleagues try to cover up for him but the lunches became longer and longer and his work hours become shorter and shorter. What time he does put in becomes so error strewn that everything he accomplishes has to be checked. His home life deteriorates at the same time. After the normal procedures and warnings are carefully followed, he is fired.

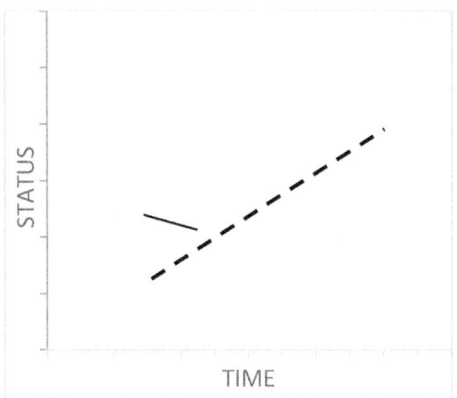

<u>Employment Plot for the Alcoholic</u>

<u>Commentary</u> Arthur is a sad case, uncommon but not rare. His Occupation Track promises a successful vocation in the Finance department. Unfortunately, his Career Path declines: his Skills deteriorate and the gap between those Skills and his Wealth and Esteem shrinks (his Wealth is unlikely to diminish so the reduction will be in Esteem). He is fired even before he reaches the expected ZSP, the balance point between Skills and Wealth and Esteem.

## 5.9 Conclusions and Chapter's Key Points

In this chapter we have reflected on all Classes of Career Paths with Inclined Occupation Plots, the most common type in management. Hopefully readers will belong to the popular category of Inclined Career Paths within an Organisation that offers Inclined Occupation Tracks. In the same spirit we will continue in the next two chapters to learn about Level and Declining Occupation Tracks with their related Classes of Career Paths.

Employment Plots with Inclining Occupation Tracks are the choice of the aspiring as they offer the opportunity to increase Wealth & Esteem

With Inclined Occupation Tracks, Inclined Career Paths are needed to demonstrate escalating Skills and to achieve the potential growth in Wealth & Esteem

Even with Inclined Occupation Tracks, increases in Wealth & Esteem are limited with Level Career Paths

Declining Career Paths will not be helped by Inclining Occupation Tracks

# CHAPTER 6 REGULAR LEVEL OCCUPATION TRACKS

## 6.1. Introduction

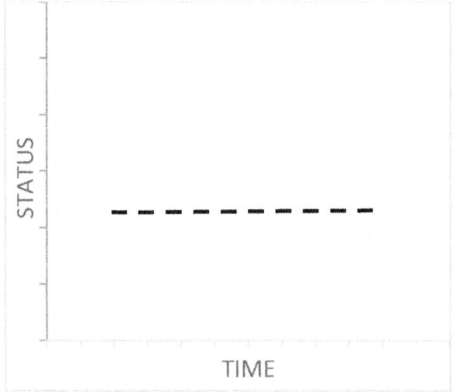

<u>Model Employment Plot With Level Occupation Track</u>

We can now move on from Inclined to **Level** Occupation Tracks. Although this Class could appear to be of less interest than that of the Inclined Tracks beloved of management students, it is significant because it covers a great many workers. Level Tracks are **not hierarchical** since there is no comparative Status above or below. Employees fall into two main sets;

What I call **Group Employed**: the large part of the labour force that work at the same job throughout their working life.

The **self-employed** who, by definition, are not in competition with anyone else in an Organisation. Think of tradespeople, artists, small shop proprietors or buskers.

As usual, we will consider all the three Classes of Career Paths within the Employment Plots (bold lines in the Plots) involving Level Occupation Tracks (dotted lines) and I will offer a couple of examples, one from each of the above sets (Group and Self Employed).

## 6.2 Regular Inclined Career Paths

### Case Study: In the Royal Principality (Group Employed)

Dai hails from the Principality of Wales. For those who gave up Geography at school at the first opportunity (good choice, I would say) Wales is a sort of country on the West side of Great Britain. There is a love/hate relationship between Wales and the rest of the Kingdom: the Welsh hate all the other British and those other British love the idea of Wales (if only they knew where it was.)

Until recently, the main industry in Wales was coal mining, now fast disappearing. The most common job was that of miner itself, involving hacking away at the coal buried deep underground with only a canary to help with Health and Safety.

Miners' sons became miners (miners' daughters were exempt) as primogeniture was a powerful instinct that overcame a sensible reluctance to earn a living in such harsh circumstances. In addition, there were few other occupations available; you could become a union official, but that vocation was only available to miners, so that was a Catch 22. **All** miners were extremely good singers, but since everybody was talented in that direction opportunities were few and far between. In addition, breaking ranks and leaving the mine to get other work was frowned upon by those left behind.

I make this employment sound horrific; in fact, despite the harsh environment, miners were the life blood of Great Britain and deserve the utmost respect.

Commentary

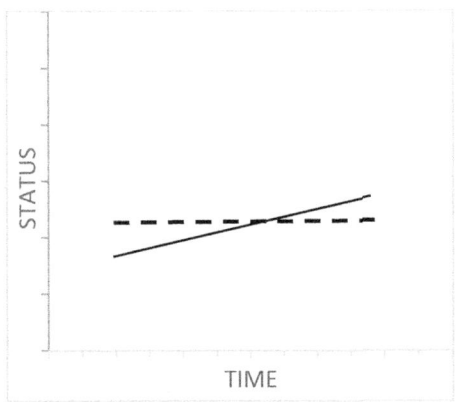

Employment Plot of Dai the Miner

The Organisation is the local pit; this will offer many sorts of Occupation Tracks including Inclined (management) and Declined (pit pony fettlers) but the only one available to Dai is "miner". Within his "gang" there will be a hierarchy dependent on each individual's Work, but our perspective is that of the management (after all, they do pay the wages) and from their point of view Dai is just one of an amorphous lump of labour with no distinctions amongst them of Wealth & Esteem.

Dai "went down the mine" when he left school aged sixteen and worked there until he retired early as his strength was broken. He began and ended his Career doing the same job as a miner; during that time his Skills increased a little through experience, but this improvement was not rewarded by higher Wealth & Esteem.

I am guessing that Dai's type of employment makes up the majority. Those of us who write and read organization theory often forget that most of humanity, especially in the "Third World", do not have the luxury of choosing their Careers.

## Case Study:  The Lady with the Lamp (Self Employed)

No, not the British one, the American one. The Statue of Liberty. She has stood as a bastion of freedom at the entrance to the US of A since 1886; so far so good, and it is expected that she will continue her steadfast presence for some time yet.

> "Give me your tired, your poor,
>
> Your huddled masses yearning to break free
>
> The wretched refuse of your teeming shore."

(*The New Colossus, a sonnet by Emma Lazarus*)

She was a gift from France (the Statue of Liberty, not Emma) who had established a tradition of Liberty, Equality and Fraternity at around the time of their biggest revolution in 1789 (didn't that go well?) and who thought that this gave them the right to sermonise to everyone else.

She has given birth to hundreds of replicas around the world but no one knows who the father(s) is/are. From her berthing her reputation has blossomed, particularly during the period of mass immigration to the States.

A visit to nearby Ellis Island tells you much more about the glories of America than crawling up the insides of the Lady to jostle in a tiny overcrowded room with a restricted view of nothing but the sea.

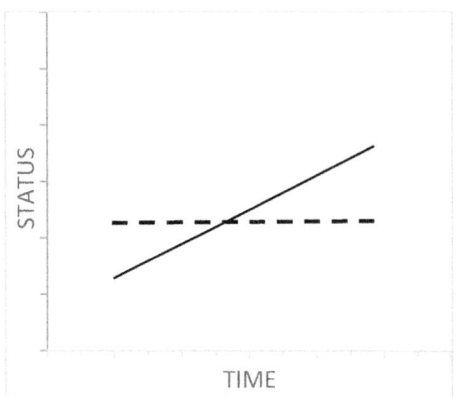

Employment Plot for the Statue of Liberty

Commentary The Organisation is the world of statuary, though I am tempted to assign this Plot to French Practical jokes - a very specialist field. As part of statuary this puts our Lady in the same arena as those massive Buddhas and Mount Rushmore. The Lady's Skills are limited, through her value has grown steadily with the price of copper (her weight is around 200 tons, current copper price @£200/ton = £100,000) and, some say, she still acts as a symbol for her new country despite being an immigrant. She is not in a hierarchy as no one statue really is better than another and the replicas are not exactly competition.

Wealth & Esteem have not, on average, changed, much over the years; some say it is better now than when she landed and others decry her symbolism. She does, however, stand as a reminder to all solo individuals casting their talents on to the marketplace that our Occupation Track is as much likely to be Level as Inclined, despite our confidence in our Skills.

# 6.3 Regular Level Career Paths

Case Study: Brothers in Arms (Group)

Two brothers named Mr. A+ and Mr. B- lived side by side in semi-detached houses on a small estate with very similar furnishings and equipment. Both had loving wives who worked all day and young sons who both went to the same school. In fact, the brothers took it in turns to do the school run. They got on really well and always had done from childhood. They were proud of their families and of being house-husbands.

From both outside and inside the homes looked much of a muchness, but underneath things were different: Mr. A+ was over-the-top house proud but Mr. B- was definitely not. Their approach to housework was like chalk and cheese. Mr. A+ (who lived in the right-hand house as you look at it) did not just dust, he polished every surface every day. Mr. B- only dusted when he could see the offensive detritus and only polished visible surfaces on high days and holidays. Mr. A+ did his washing daily with every ungent known to man, Mr. B- washed with just the basics. Mr. A+ ironed everything (even underwear) and spent most of a morning folding the clothing to Gap stores standards. Mr. B- took a more rough and ready approach. Mr. A+ washed all the dishes before stacking the dishwasher and put it on every day. Mr. B- chucked the dirty plates in and only started it up when it was over-full. Mr. A+ took an hour to clean the lavatories, Mr. B- considerably less, if at all. Mr. A+ vacuumed under the furniture, Mr. B- around it. Mr. A+ had a strict weekly routine; Mr. B- did not plan and did his housework when the fancy took him.

Commentary

Employment Plot for the Brothers

The Organisation is basic requirements of living; the Occupation Plot is housework. I am going to go out on a limb here and provide perhaps perspectives that may be different to yours. Notice is drawn to the relatively high Organisation plot. This is because I, at least, regard the Wealth (the cost of a cleaner or au pair) to be noteworthy and the Esteem to be much higher than the general image of chores. Notice is also drawn to the closeness of Mr. A+'s Career plot (the upper one) and Mr. B-'s (the lower one), despite the fact that the Skills and application of Mr. A+ are significantly better than those of Mr. B-. This is because the pertinent perspectives on the housework are those of their wives, who do not mind any differences. Perhaps, once in a while, they could help out, but that would make a hierarchy of two in each household and there are no guesses as to who would be on top.

You will probably complain, if you are like me, that your abilities and effort go unrecognized compared to those of your colleagues. This is because the important thing is that the job is done, not how well it is done. Take comfort in the fact that promotion is based on demonstrating the Skills of the next step up on the ladder, not those of your present rung

Case Study:  Writers' Block (Self Employed)

An author's life is not a happy one. Toiling by day and night the muse is often away with the fairies. Harassed by children, nagged by wife, scorned by friends and reviled by an illiterate public, he spends many hours in self-doubt. Seeing his last opus languishing in the remainders' pile in the local bookshop casts depression and anxiety. No one gives him credit for being the first writer to successfully split an infinitive (esoteric joke).

Only his faith in his abilities keeps him going. He cogitates on all of his fellow scribblers in the past who went unrecognized in their own lifetimes. What makes him really angry are the bestsellers churned out by unschooled hacks. Was it for this that he did his Master's degree in Creative Writing? Was it for this that he gave up that sinecure in the Marketing Department?

Perhaps he should change his genre? With all that experience in the Marketing Department he could write a bestseller on Organisation Theory, possibly around the idea of Status and Employment? There must be a market for that sort of thing.

If only he can keep going. Then the rewards for his undoubted gifts will materialize. Only then will the truth be out, royalties flood in and his burial spot in Poets' Corner in Westminster Abbey be secured.

## Commentary

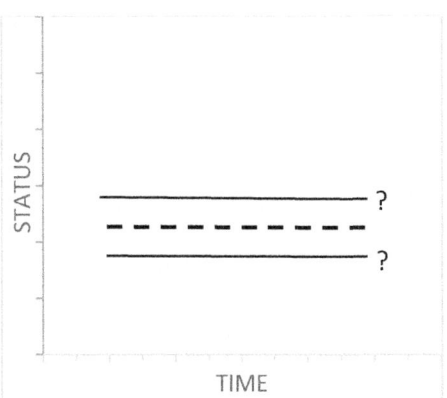

STATUS

TIME

Employment Plot for an Author

I do not suppose that the situation our author finds himself in will bring tears to your eyes. Nearer the mark, perhaps, would be a sense of regret that you purchased this epistle, but hopefully better is to come.

The Organisation is the hostile world of publishing, the Occupation Track is for fiction writers.

I have provided two possible Career Paths in the above Employment Plot, one for the author's own perspective on his Skills and the other for that of his wife. Guess which one is which!

All too often we, especially the self-employed, continue to plough a furrow when all the signs are that we will not succeed; but then all those who do succeed started off that way.

## 6.4  Regular Declining Career Paths

I guess that we must face it: sometimes our Skills deteriorate and our Career Paths decline. Just because this is unfortunate does not mean that we should ignore such scenarios. Rather than averting your eyes, I am sure you want to be brave for the sake of a thorough review of Occupation Tracks.

Case Study:  London's Finest (Group)

A Cockney gentleman "does the knowledge". For those unfamiliar with this examination it involves a trial for potential London black cab drivers (aka "cabbies"). In this test our candidate is rigorously quizzed on the best routes around London to get from one location to another, plus the whereabouts of every restaurant, hotel, tourist spot and any other place a cab customer is likely to ask for.

It is one of the hardest tests that a person can undertake and budding cabbies often spend years traipsing around the capital, usually on mopeds, memorising every detail. Doctorate vivas are a cinch compared with this examination.

Our candidate is successful at his third attempt and begins his Career in a secondhand cab. The remainder of his working life is spent in this trade. As time passes his memory lapses sporadically and he gets a little out of date. He occasionally needs a Satnav which is carefully concealed from his customers who, of course, supply his Esteem. London traffic gets worse and worse and, I regret to say, he takes his feelings out verbally. The high standards that he began with all bright eyed and bushy-tailed decline a fraction and, against the rules, he refuses to take some clients "South of the River". Despite this, our cabbie and his peers are one of the three best things about London (the other two are the BBC and pubs).

Commentary

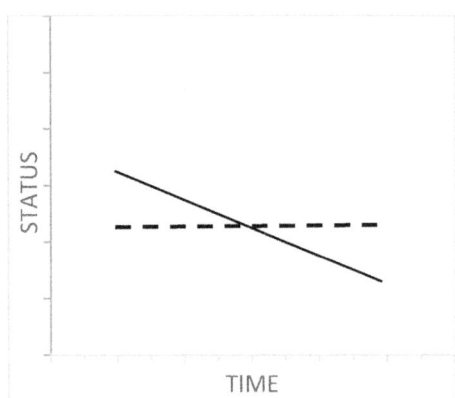

Employment Plot for a Cabbie

The Organisation is the Licensed Taxi Trade Association, the Occupation Track is taxi driving which was, and remains, a necessity in the Capital. Despite the emergence of web-based competition, the black cab's trade has stayed steady-as-she-goes for years. Our Cockney's reputation originally stayed high with very high Skills which earn him adequate Wealth and high Esteem from all Londoners and especially tourists who compare his Skill with equivalent cab drivers in their own countries. However, as with many who earn a living on their own, standards and Esteem shrink with time.

In Some Organisations there are many of us whose talents actually diminish with age relative to our younger colleagues. Experience does not always balance the advantages of youth. Our cabbie and his ilk have not developed their Skills in the changing circumstances.

Case Study: Famous for Being Famous (Self Employed)

Gloria was famous for being famous. She was a "celebrity." How she got to this eminent height is something of a mystery, especially to herself. A good start was to have a figure best described as "noteworthy" and a face that was not. A second stage in her canonization was extensive self-promotion on social media. A third step was to date a man in the same walk of life as the lady in question.

The real factor, we suspect, was simple chance. A chunk of our humanity seems to need exaggerated icons that they can both admire and dislike at the same time. Celebrity culture is endemic but that is not to say that it is somehow dreadful.

Gloria hates paparazzi but lives by their exertions; never knowingly undersold she is never pictured by them in anything other than full war paint. What lies underneath is anyone's guess.

She is in a symbiotic relationship with a press that is dedicated to their mutual plugging. The fees she earns from them smother any doubts she may have as to their embarrassing contents.

Commentary

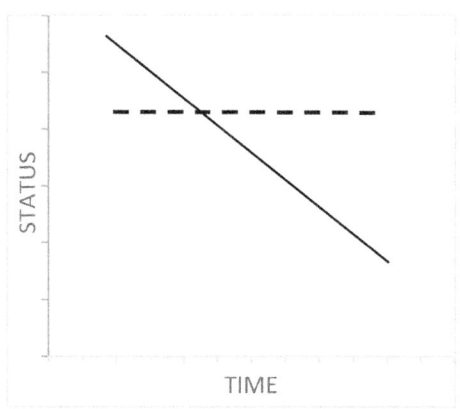

Employment Plot for a Celebrity

The Organisation is the Popular Media, the Occupation Track is Female Icons. Gloria will rocket into the starry firmament and fade, the sparks to be re-lit by the next cohort. Renowned for now, we sympathisers just hope that the dosh lasts a little time longer as she disappears from whence she came. Meanwhile we can only wonder at how little talent earns such a superstar prestige. Those ladies (and gentlemen, though perhaps fewer) who wish to emulate Gloria will all aspire to a Career Path that does not decline and will, in fact, Incline. They may well be disappointed, but at least for a little time, their Wealth & Esteem will be greater than that of our author above.

## 6.5  Conclusions and Chapter Key Points

Regular Level Occupation Tracks are all around us; they do not offer the obvious advantages (if you can take them) of Inclining Tracks, but there are still opportunities to pursue a declined Career Path against Level Occupation Tracks with, perhaps, less competition.

Self Employment (a characteristic form of Level Occupation Track models since there is no hierarchy), is often a route to earning one's living exercised by necessity rather than by choice. Here the competition comes not from your business colleagues but from your rivals in the same trade. Here too, however there is a direct link between Skills and Wealth & Esteem.

**Regular Level Occupation Tracks can apply to groups of workers and the self-employed.**

**All three Classes of Career Paths can and do interlink with Level Occupation Tracks.**

**Opportunities in Organisations that offer Level Occupation Tracks are likely to be fewer than for Inclining Tracks but competition is also likely to be less.**

# CHAPTER 7  REGULAR DECLINING OCCUPATION TRACKS

## 7.1  Introduction

I fear that we must turn our attention to the last of the three Classes of Occupation Tracks: those that provide declining Wealth & Esteem over time.

Fortunately, these are not common and, although they are depressing, they are included here firstly to ensure that all types of Organisation are comprehensively covered and secondly to show this Class as a warning of what your fate might be.

Again, I will cover this Class of Occupation Track with examples of the three Classes of Career Paths (Inclined, Level and Declined) but will only give one of each to prevent us from becoming too morose.

## 7.2  Regular Inclined Career Paths

### Case Study:  The Reverend

A young priest is welcomed to his first parish. Fresh from his seminary he is a touch naïve at the start, but the rough and tumble of a deprived area soon hardens him. Over the years of his service he becomes more and more respected and his advice and aptitude for consolation are increasingly sought after.

Sadly, demand for the sacraments drops: baptisms go out of fashion, weddings are held at registry offices without blessings, and funerals move to humanist commemorations. His flock decays, with the elderly dying and fewer births of potential worshipers. His prayers provide consolation but the collection plate contents diminish month by month.

The Bishop is too involved in diocese affairs and is too grand to be bothered with his actual parishes and offers nothing but prayers. Our priest feels that he is left to his own devices; happily, the comfort and succour that he affords his flock demonstrate his flair for charity. Certainly, his stipend never grows at the same rate as his responsibilities.

Commentary

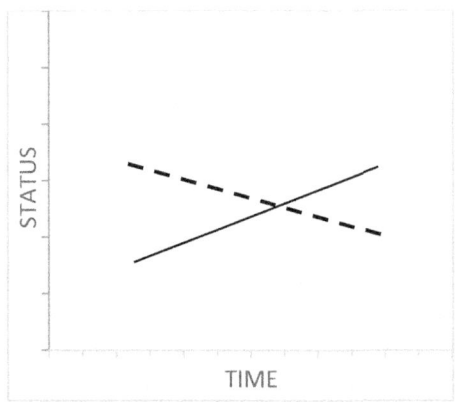

Employment Plot for The Reverend

The Organisation is the Church, the Occupation Track is that for a clergyman struggling against the falling demands for his ecclesiastical services.

Our Reverend increases his Skills during his tenure but Wealth & Esteem drop. We should not forget the Life Status opportunities for him, which I suspect, are more than sufficient compensation.

Whether the same could be said for you in such circumstances I will leave you to decide.

## 7.3 Regular Level Career Paths

### Case Study: Perils of the Sea

The wind howled, the storm raged, the tempest boiled. Lightning lit and thunder thundered. The ship battled against the elements but survival seemed impossible. The crew hung on for dear life praying to their Gods for deliverance.

Suddenly it looked as if these prayers were answered, but we do not know which God was the effective one. On the rocks emerged three mermaids who reclined bewitchingly (on land they could not do anything other than recline.) These were not at all like Hans Christian Anderson's "Little Mermaid". They were, shall we say, a bit more mature and enticing. Their seductive wails pierced the cataclysm tantalizing the sailors. Their siren calls floated above crashing waves.

Many of the distressed sailors were highly desirous of the offers and their appetites grew when the mermaids held up a sign saying "Special Offer Three for Two". Some of the seamen were attracted by the feminine charms on display, others who were starving licked their lips at the prospect of Surf 'n' Turf on one spit roast carcass. Only one of our nautical brethren rejoiced at the prospect of salvation.

The Captain, having been educated beyond the basics and able to read and write (a bit), knew but little of mythology and the dangers of sea nymphs. "Me first", he yelled as he plunged into the foaming brine and to his death.

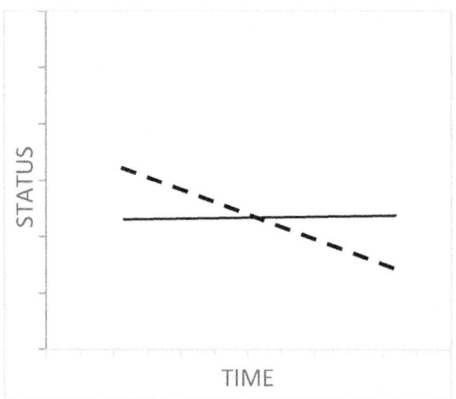

Employment Plot for Mermaids

Commentary The Organisation is mythology, the Occupation Track is tempting sailors to their demise. The Status and the function of mermaids has declined significantly since ships advanced from sail to steam; shipwrecks are less common and, when they do happen, they frequently spill oil (which mermaids hate because it messes with their hair). They are still about, nevertheless. Seldom seen but, as do all good myths, they remain useful for scaring kids.

The mermaids' Skills have remained constant over the years but their Esteem has declined with their lack of opportunity to ply their trade. I am not sufficiently expert to comment on their Wealth.

Recognise when your business is out of date; hard to give up on the years of developing skills and investment, but often it is better to cut your losses.

## 7.4 Regular Declining Career Paths

### Case Study: The Paramour

Susie began her living as the mistress of a chap named Tommy. At first it was a very comfortable existence; he had established her in a nice flat, bought her expensive dinners, sent round flowers and showered her with presents and all for doing something that she quite enjoyed.

The first minute crack came when he brought a friend called Mike to the apartment who, in return for shared favours, gave Susie her first taste of Class A wicked medications. From then on Mike, and later others, were frequent visitors, always bringing more and more interesting substances. Naturally, Tommy moved on to fresher pastures, turfing Susie out of the flat to make room for a newer model.

Susie, by now addicted to heroin, became a "hostess" in a "Gentlemen's Club", then moved down to a high-class brothel, then low class and then the streets. The last I heard Tommy was OK.

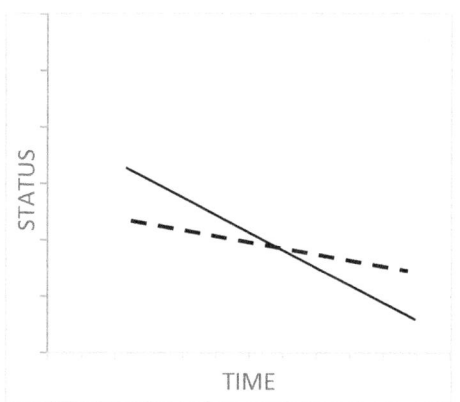

Employment Plot for the Paramour

Commentary The Organisation is the sex trade, the Career Path is essentially that of a prostitute, though that is not what Suzie intended when she first met Tommy. The Wealth & Esteem of Suzie's profession is in decline due in part to the availability of contraception freeing up amateurs and the prevalence of pornography which is frequently cheaper. Her personal tale is steeper: Suzie's Skills deteriorate with the natural ravages of time. I do hope that you do not fall into the oldest profession. There is a lot of competition.

## 7.5 Conclusions and Chapter's Key Points

I hope, from the three examples above, that you know that Declining Occupation Tracks and the Organisations that afford them are best avoided if you have the choice. However, in these Case Studies it is clear that the Reverend, the Mermaids and Suzie did not have much say in the matter and once cast in their roles it was very difficult to escape.

**If at all possible, avoid Declining Occupation Tracks**

# CHAPTER 8  MICRO ASPECTS OF REGULAR EMPLOYMENT PLOTS

## 8.1 Introduction

The Employment Plots considered so far have had long timescales, usually the working life of the subject. As a result, the Career Paths and Organisation Tracks are smooth lines with no variations. Clearly there will be discrepancies year by year, month by month and even hour by hour. You are now invited to put a magnifying glass to three Employment Plots to see how "spikes" can happen day to day.

## 8.2 Negative Spikes in Employment Plots

### Case Study:  Dr. Cure

Dr. Cure, a doctor in General Practice, is holding her morning surgery and is faced with the customary complaints of coughs and colds, baby rashes, hypochondria and erectile dysfunctions. A new patient, a Mr. Werewolf, is invited in and he explains his ailments.

About once a month, he says, he has the same vivid dream that he is a rabid dog whose tail has been docked. "It's really real," he describes his terrors, "It is as if I actually was there in the forest. After the nightmares I am weak and debilitated for days".

Dr. Cure examines Mr. Werewolf. She Googles the symptoms discreetly but cannot get past "Monthly Problems" whose indicators certainly do not apply to the hirsute Mr. Werewolf.

I am afraid to say that Dr. Cure missed evident signs shown by her patient such as the meeting of his eyebrows over the bridge of his nose. She advises him that she is unsure (i.e. baffled in health professional circles) and will refer him to a specialist.

Before we leave our tale of Dr. Cure (who is the subject of this Case Study) I am sure that you would want to know what happened to Mr. Werewolf. Well, he spiraled around several medical experts including a psychiatrist, tried acupuncture and yoga and even resorted to vegetarianism, but his dreams continued once a month. By luck he chanced upon a vet who easily diagnosed lycanthropy and offered to put Mr. Werewolf down as long as he paid in advance. As it happened, Mr. Werewolf's next dream involved chasing a cat and he was run over by a car and did not wake up.

Commentary

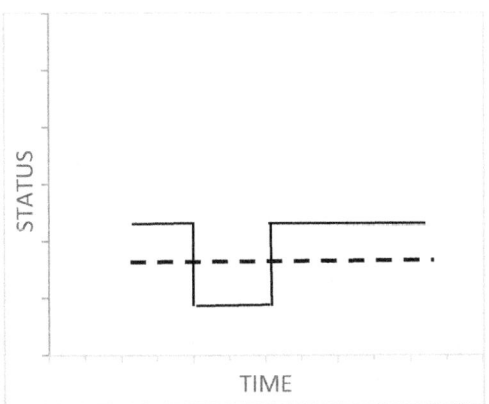

Employment Plot for Dr. Cure Showing Forty Minute Spike

N.B. Plot Time Scale = 9.30 – 11.30. on a Tuesday

Dr. Cure was sailing along practising her Skills when Mr. Werewolf turned up. During his consultation and examination she failed **for a**

**short period** to live up to her normal standards as required by her Hippocratic oath. This would not show up in her full Employment plot over her working life. However, one swallow does not a summer make, thank goodness. It is the "smoothed" Career Path that you will be judged on, not those unfortunate little incidents, as long as they are recovered from.

## 8.3 Positive Spikes in Employment Plots

### Case Study: The Law Officer

Jim applied to be a British police officer straight after leaving university. He was accepted, completed his training and joined the Metropolitan force as a constable. The first year or two were routine: a lot of desk work, a bit of riot control, a bit of sweeping up drunks (not his colleagues), separating fighting neighbours, or arresting anybody who got in the way. No pavement plodding, that is out of fashion.

After a period of time into his routine lowly ranking, he was off duty and in his bank asking for another overdraft when two armed bank robbers crashed in. Jim immediately attacked, pinning one of the robbers down while the other shot him and fled. Despite his wound Jim hung on to the miscreant until help arrived and he was taken to hospital. The wound was not serious and he recovered after some recuperation and came back to work. He was commended for his bravery (foolhardiness?), given a police medal and promoted to Detective Sergeant.

Some time later Jim was occupied on a murder case when, by complete accident, he fell over the vital clue to the killer's identity. Obviously this was presented to his superiors as a flash of inspiration due entirely to his forensic talents. The felon was convicted and sentenced for a long stretch. Jim acquired another commendation, another medal and another promotion to Detective Inspector.

Commentary

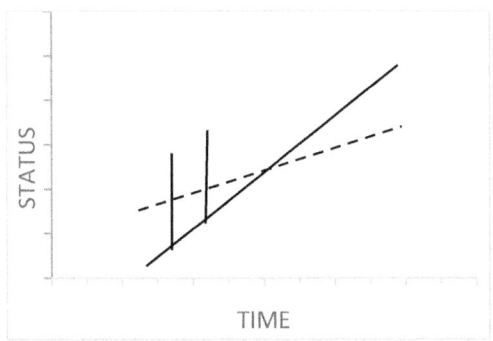

Employment Plot for The Law Officer Showing Two Spikes

Jim was following the normal Career Plot for the Organisation of the Metropolitan Police when, on two very brief occasions, his Skills spiked, leading to promotion "up the ladder" at a faster rate than he could have expected. Please note that the accidental events **drove** his preferment; if they had not transpired he would have risen in the ranks at a slower pace. Compare with:

Case Study:  The Professional

Gary loved golf from the first time his father gave him a cut down club. He left school as soon as was legal and spent every waking hour on the course, on the range and on the putting green. Soon, an amateur champion, he took his exams, became a junior professional and joined the local circuit.

Happily Gary was one of the very few to make it. He played in more and more serious competitions, appointed a long- term caddy and began to earn sufficient prize monies to have a good life, to marry and to start a family. But this was not good enough, Gary wanted to win and win big. Sure enough, as his practice reaped the benefits, he did win major tournaments and even an open championship. Gary had succeeded where so many have failed.

Commentary

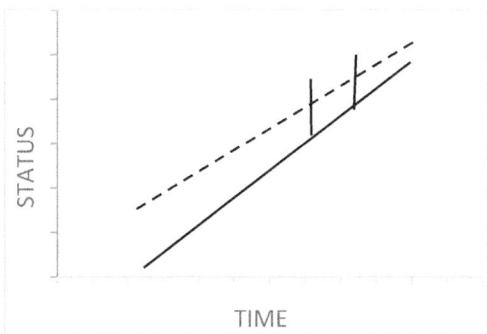

Employment Plot for The Professional Showing Spikes for Major Wins

Gary would only consider a major win as a spike. Anything less, even coming second, would only be par for the course (joke!). Those major triumphs were few and far between, but for him, his Dad and his fans, they formed his Career and its plot.

In contrast to our Law Officer the Career spikes came about as the **result** of the steady inclination of the Career Path and were not its **driving force**.

It is a fortunate fact of life that positive spikes in Employment Plots tend to have greater significance than the negative ones.

## 8.4 Conclusion and Chapter's Key Points

Spikes will happen in all Careers; let us hope that they are positive or that nobody notices the negatives. Yet Careers need to be observed through a telescope from the wrong end, not a microscope, with aberrations and shocks smoothed into the total.

**All Careers will have Good and Bad Spikes**

**Take advantage of the good and blame others for the bad**

# CHAPTER 9  IRREGULAR EMPLOYMENT PLOTS

## 9.1 Introduction

All the Employment plots discussed so far have **linear** plots for both Careers and Organisations. However, there are many types of Organisations that do not fit this pattern and this chapter outlines a few of these. The examples below are by no means a comprehensive or exhaustive list.

With a bit of creativity we can stretch simple Employment Plots to represent many diverse Organisations; you will, no doubt, be able to think of more classes and better examples.

## 9.2 Blocked Employment Plots

Blocked Employment plots are when what might be seen as a normal progression up the Career line is blocked and the individual cannot advance further, thus becoming stuck. There are two types: overt and mythical.

### Case Study : Brothers in Arms

Travis comes from a long line of service in the Royal Dragoon Guards, a regiment of the Line Cavalry in the British army. His father and his grandfather and, I guess, ancestors going even further back, were all in the regiment and rose to high ranks therein. Following in their footsteps Travis enrolled in the University Officers' Training Corps and (surprise surprise) was selected to train at Sandhurst at the interview with the Army Officer Selection Board. After the requisite education he "passed out" and began his proper Career as a First Lieutenant.

In slight contrast Trevor did not have a family history of killing people (at least not legally) but was tough, intelligent and ambitious. In this respect he exceeded the officer Travis. He always wanted to be a soldier so he applied at his local Army Recruitment Office and was successful, as was everyone who was foolish enough to enter that office. Trevor was different to your average squaddie; over the years he worked extremely hard in very tough tests and rapidly advanced up six ranks; eventually, after many years, reaching the top of the non-commission tree as Warrant Officer Class 2. There he stopped. The chances of escalating just to the bottom of the officer class, where Travis started his career, were effectively forbidden. Meanwhile Travis had climbed only around halfway up his twelve possible ranks to Lieutenant Colonel.

Travis and Trevor rarely met. They ate and drank in different messes. Travis spent most of his time in an office, Trevor out in the wilds training his men.

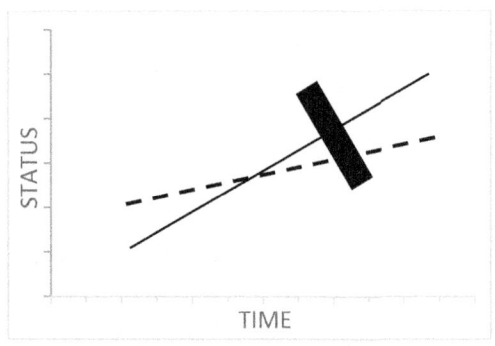

Employment Plot for Trevor

Commentary  The British army is like all other military bodies, highly hierarchical. The men and women have to wear insignia so that there can be no confusion as to who is above whom. Recognition of rank must be made absolutely evident by the ritual of saluting. Trevor begins his time in the army as Incompetent but soon is much more Competent than Travis (not shown). Trevor is **blocked** from making any further headway, nor even to reach the level at which Travis started. The block is **overt** since everyone knows that it exists, is quite open about it and does nothing about it. Not good.

You should be able to determine whether or not a potential Career is Overtly Blocked due to its obvious character; recognize what it is for what it is and do not complain if and when you do not get over the block. You chose the system, and the system chose you on the understanding that your choice was informed as to the nature of its careers.

## Case Study: High Flyer

Virginia had done everything that could possibly be asked of her: first class degree in PPE, a further degree in Law and an MBA from a top Ivy League university. She began her professional vocation at a boutique management consultancy Sky Blue Visionaries. She was immensely successful, in the beginning working on projects led by senior staff but soon taking on the control of assignments herself.

She deliberately subjugated her personal life to her employment; she did not marry and had no significant other. No children and even no cat. Virginia was very popular with her staff giving clear direction and credit where it was due. Although it was the firm's Partners' responsibility to find new customers, her clients now always asked for her to run their ventures and she built up a strong portfolio through their recommendations. She was a leading member of their trade body and was well known and respected throughout the entire industry.

What nobody could understand was why she was never made a Partner in Sky Blue Visionaries. Although well remunerated, in the form of a salary and bonuses, the real caboodles came from the profit share amongst the Partners and, despite promises made and polite pats on the head at her glowing appraisals, that goal was elusive.

The rumour was that her lack of elevation to the sunny vistas was because she was a woman! It did not escape her attention that all the Partners were men and not one of them was from a minority background. Virginia persuaded the Human Resources department to organise Gender Awareness Training for all staff including the Partners, who naturally did not notice that the effort was aimed at them.

Eventually Virginia left Sky Blue Visionaries and set up her own practice taking her clients with her.

Commentary

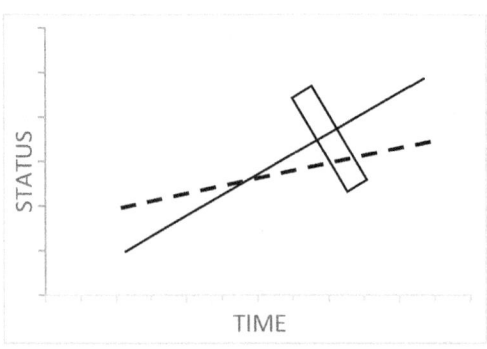

Employment Plot for the High Flyer

As in the Case Study above, Virginia is **blocked** in her Career by what is commonly known as "The Glass Ceiling" where staff from a minority (women were a minority at Sky Blue Visionaries) are prevented from ascending the ladder past a certain point, banging their heads against that barrier, while those comfortably above look down. In contrast to the blocked **overt** scenario this is called blocked **mythical,** since everyone above the ceiling conveniently thinks that this form of blocking is a myth.

All I can advise is that you do as Virginia does and move on. Dinosaurs are exceptionally stubborn as well as exceptionally stupid.

## 9.3 Exponential and Logarithmic Employment Plots

So far we have analysed our model Career and Organisation plots that are straight lines i.e. are linear progressions. Obviously we can have lots of different shapes for both Career Paths and Occupation Tracks. I have three examples below where either the Career or the Occupation Track is **exponentially** or **logarithmically** drawn whilst the other is linear. This type of Employment Plot is of special interest because the two lines can **cross twice**!

Case Study: Treading the Boards

Sir Archibald Foster began his acting profession when he was cast as the donkey in his first school nativity play. Not for the first time he thought that the polite applause from all the loving parents was all due to him. From then on he was hooked and, to be fair, he was very good at it.

After senior school plays and further encouragement, he attended the premier acting academy. His first paid job was as an understudy to the Bear in "The Winter's Tale". Slowly but surely he hustled his way through a packed field and began to get a reputation as a

Shakespearean specialist who was able to make you understand some semblance of the plot, if not any of the actual lines. He avoided the pitfalls of celebrity goings-on and the filthy lucre of fronting television advertising but did grace the box with his tragic declamations from the bard.

Being openly gay necessitated his knighthood but he encouraged his fellow thespians to address him as plain Archie. Everyone raved about his Hamlet and then, in due course of time, his Othello, his starring part in the Scottish play and then his Lear. Archie was much in demand on interview programmes and had two books on the theatre ghost written under his name.

Then things changed: he became too well loved and respected, became a national institution, became a "luvvie". He had descended from acting to acting out acting. Rapidly he grew into a bit of a laughingstock. Productions of the ageless dramatist no longer suited his habit of hogging the stage. Last we heard of him was in a green room declaring, "My dears! You should have seen my Donkey! Tears in their eyes, my dears, tears in their eyes!"

Commentary

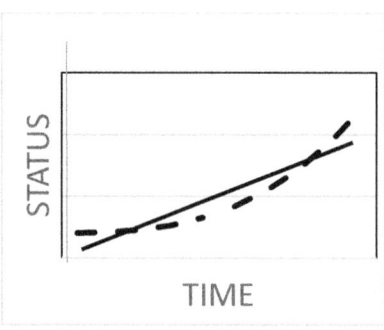

Employment Plot for Sir Archibald Foster

Ladies and Gentlemen! Roll up roll up for the double crossing of Career and Organisation plots! The rare exponential growth of an Organisation Track combined with a linear Career Path allows Sir Archie to move over time from Incompetent as a young budding actor through a Competent phase and finally into Incompetent again.

Self-satisfaction in careers can lead to hubris and, as day follows night, a fall!

## Case Study: Dennis the Arachnid

Robert the Bruce, a Scottish King of sorts, set off on his own to hunker down for the winter in a cave, because Hiltons had not been invented in the fourteenth century. He could have stayed with the MacDonalds and dined superbly, but they were off to see their sister. The fact is that Robert wanted to be alone; he had not had the best of years fighting the Sassenachs and he was sulking. No one was brave enough to say it out loud but basically he was on the run.

Legend has it that being ever so bored, he noticed a spider and paid it some attention; the spider was trying to build a web (so it is surmised) and was trying to spin a first line between two rocks. Robert christened the Spider Dennis after his uncle who was usually legless. The cynics amongst you will claim that spiders do not spin webs in the winter, as there are few insects flying about to get trapped in webs at that time of the year. Also, spiders hibernate. Perhaps it was a very mild winter or perhaps the spider was just practising. Such quibbles have nothing to do with the thrust of the legend.

My guess is that the cold got to Dennis because he was pretty useless at casting this first line. Alternative diagnoses are a possible sprained ankle or that he just did not feel like it. He would fix the line on a bottom rock but drop it as he scrambled up to his chosen elevated anchor. Time after time he scuttled up and down with no success. Eventually his exercises had warmed him up and, at last, the footing was secured, but he was so tired that he fell asleep and when he woke up, he had forgotten all about it.

Robert had been entranced! "If at first you don't succeed – try, try, try again!" His consequent battle against the English at Bannockburn was so brilliant that all Scots will try to bring it into any conversation you might have with them.

Commentary

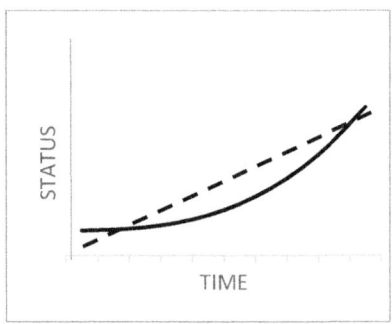

STATUS

TIME

<u>Employment Plot for Dennis the Spider</u>

Here we have the mirror of the Case Study above with an exponential Career Path combined with a linear Occupation Track. Our arachnid starts off his hopeful web building exercise as a competent little spider but then falls short in his work, only to become competent again through his repeated exertions.

Robert's observations on reiteration and subsequent fortune should be taken to heart by us all.

Case Study: The Genius

Wolfgang Amadeus Mozart was an infant prodigy. He could play "Chopsticks" all the way through with only a couple of mistakes before he was weaned. All he wanted for Christmas was his own fortepiano (the same as a pianoforte but black and white keys reversed). He was a maestro on both the violin and keyboards by the time he was five, which meant that he could play both parts of his string sonatas simultaneously. Wolfgang's tutor was a Viennese hack famous for quantity rather than quality, a trick he had learnt from big Bach and all the little Bachs.

His father campaigned vigorously to puff his virtuoso son, presenting him to royalty (of which there was quite a lot around) throughout Europe, pretending Wolfgang was six when he was seven. In contrast, Mozart pater made his son dress up like an adult doll with a wig and all.

Wolfgang soon fled the nest and fell into the bad company of a writer called Da Ponte who persuaded him to help compose three naughty operas, which they got away with because they were in Italian and nobody in Vienna got the dirty jokes.

After his "precocious" and "crazy" periods (whose zenith was a piano sonata in E flat minor, deliberately lost) he settles into his maturity grinding out symphonies (41) and piano concertos (23) and lots of bits and pieces.

Towards the end of his short life he got very sulky with a new boy on the block named Beethoven who only composed things in fortissimo so he could hear them. Mozart became very depressed by the Beethoven cult and he decided that the best way of preserving his legacy was to die mysteriously, leaving an enigmatic half-penned Requiem Mass amongst the half-eaten breakfast on his desk. He should have been patient and waited for the invention of Hi Fi and CDs.

Although Wolfgang reckoned himself a failure and out of fashion, in fact no musical composer before or since has topped him. Not even Wagner or those Strauss twins. Not even Simon and Garfunkel. With regard to the way so called "classical music" has been going recently, neither will anyone yet to come.

Commentary

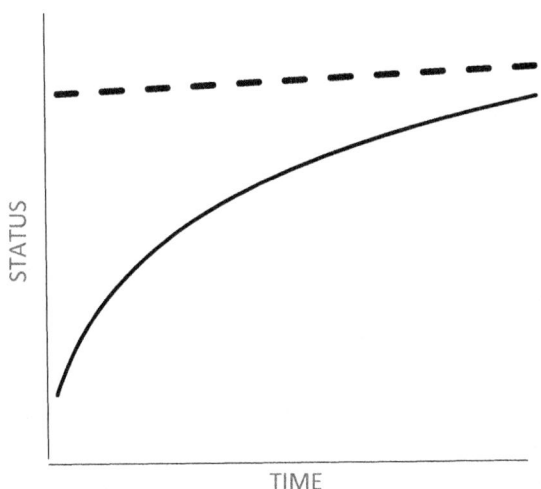

Employment Plot for Wolfgang Amadeus Mozart

Our third example in this segment is different to the two just previous: firstly the Career Path illustrated is logarithmic and secondly it does not cross with the linear Occupation Track.

Our genius rises very rapidly from his boyhood, but then levels off in later life. In his own estimation he never quite achieves the Status he could possibly realise; we disagree. Precociousness is no barrier to subsequent triumphs – it may even be a necessary condition.

## 9.4 Stratified Employment Plots

Our next development of Employment Plots involves the representation of **Multiple Career Paths** against just one Occupation Track. This is a convenience whereby you can compare different Career Paths, especially yours, against others.

Firstly, **Stratified** Employment Plots are those where layers of Status are fixed over the relevant time period and the population of each layer cannot rise (or fall) to other layers. These Stratified Plots are classed as **irregular** because, although the Occupation Track is Regular, the Career Paths are multiple.

Case Study: Christian Angelology

Always grateful to Wikipedia (All Hail!) and essential to this Case Study. The nine ranks of Angels are divided into three Spheres; the ranks in order are:

The First Sphere serve as the heavenly servants of God and are the Seraphim, the Cherubin and Thrones.

The Second Sphere are the heavenly governors of the creation and are the Dominions of Lordship, the Virtues or Strongholds and the Powers or Authorities.

The Third Sphere function as heavenly guides, protectors and messengers to human beings and are the Principalities or Rulers, the Archangels and the Angels. It is from this group that the Herald Angels belong, those that encouraged us to "Hark... Glory to the newborn King."

Every Angel is fixed in eternity in their rank. Since they are not allowed pride to look down on the lower echelons and are denied envy to gaze upon their superiors; they have nowhere to go other than chat amongst their fellows.

Commentary

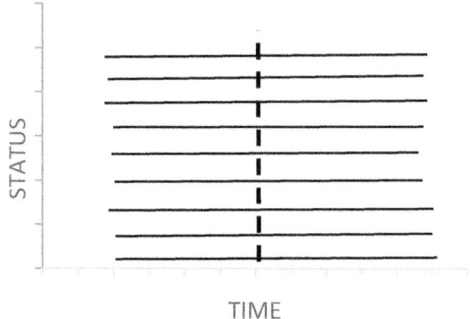

Employment Plot for the Ranks of Angels

Time Frame = Eternity

Please note the rare Vertical Occupation Track! This example picks up, as promised, on the Vertical Organisation plot, introduced in Chapter 4, signifying timelessness. All the Angels are in fixed stratified ranks and must remain so with no opportunity to rise (or fall) in Status. In practical terms, many employees feel that they are stuck at a level in their company (along with their superior and inferior colleagues) with no hope of change. This is also an example of Multiple Career Tracks on one Occupation Plot (see chapter 4.10) and with more examples now following.

Case Study: A Layman's Guide to the Orchestra and a Concert

The best way to understand the orchestra is to attend a concert. There you will find a large room divided into two, a division between you (aka the audience) and them (aka the orchestra). You should sit in the half with the most chairs but not necessarily the most people. The orchestra should have lots of participants; if there are only a handful then you are at a chamber recital and in the wrong place.

The orchestra has higher Status than the audience and are thus seated higher to demonstrate this. If the concert is in a church then they will sit at the same level as you to show appropriate humility. If they are below you and half hidden then you are at an opera. Also the wrong place and you should get out while you have the chance. Peculiarly the higher you sit in the room the lesser Status you have.

On the face of it, the group of people called an Orchestra seem to be as egalitarian and democratic as possible. Homogeneity is thy name. They call themselves a "band" and the men all dress identically and the women nearly so.

In fact the orchestra is highly stratified according to which method they use to make their noise which is called "music". In order of preference they are: sawers, blowers, hitters and shouters. You can differentiate the groups and their Status by how near the front of their bit of the room they are sitting.

First come the sawers who are nearest the front and make their music by rubbing a blunt saw against a wooden box. Each and every sawer calls his wooden box "my Stradivarius". Sometimes they join in a mass plucking of sawdust from the Stradiveri. As there are quite a lot of them they have to be further divided, ranging in importance from right to left. You can also tell their ranking by the size of their bits of wood, with the smallest coming top. On your left are a group called the "first violins" whose name signifies their pre-eminence. You can aurally pick these out as they get to play the melodies (see below). Going round clockwise, you then get to the "second violins" who are there to argue with the "first violins". Sometimes these arguments can be so bad that they have to be separated and the "second violins" are demoted to outside right.

Going round further you come to the "violas", but you need not bother with them since you cannot hear them. Furthest right come the "cellos" who, resenting their relatively lowly Status, make a sort of grumbling commotion. Right at the back are the "double basses"; you can spot these because their bigger bit of wood is taller than their sawers.

After this lot, and further back, are the blowers who are divided into those who blow straight things and those who blow curly things. The curly ones are behind the straight ones but make up for this inferior ranking by creating the most din. The curly things are shiny and the straight things are made of coloured wood, but one of the many confusing details about the orchestra is that one of the straight implements is shiny and sits with the wooden folk.

Going even further back, you get to the hitters. This group is unusual in that each hitter can swap around the various things they batter. They do not do much and spend most of the time sitting about and counting.

Last of all are the shouters. These are right at the back and sit down most of the time, only standing up to do their shouting. There have obviously been PC problems in this grouping in the past as the lady shouters have to be segregated from the gentlemen shouters.

To further complicate things each "section", as the above groups are called, has one person named the "Principal". For the hitters he or she sits alone in front of sort of large metal half eggs. For the blowers and the scrapers they are hard to find, except for the Principal of the first violins, who is so special that he gets to come out after everyone else and take a bow at the beginning of the music. The Principal of the shouters is not allowed to join in and hides in a corner until the end, when she springs to the front during the applause (see below) and you can identify her because everyone around you starts enquiring "Who's that?"

The music is made up of three constituents: melody, rhythm and counterpoint. Melody makes you want to whistle (don't), rhythm makes you want to tap your feet (don't) and counterpoint is when the different sections try to compete in making diverse melodies and rhythms. You get to choose which of these you want to listen to at any one time.

Sometimes one member of the orchestra is chosen to come to the front to make the most music in both quantity and supposed difficulty. They are called "soloists". The only hitter allowed to be a soloist is called a "Pianist" who, due to this special temporary Status, gets to hit the largest thing on the stage called a "Steinway".

One aberration stands out: he or she is called the "conductor" and their job is to control the applause. If he faces you, then you should clap and if he turns his back to you then you should stop clapping. If he walks in you should clap and if he walks out you should stop clapping. Sometimes some in the audience miss this last sign and continue with a show of appreciation and the conductor has to come in and out again, often more than once. The conductor fills in time between having to give these indications by waving their arms about. It is a common misconception that the conductor has high Status and that they choose how loud the orchestra sounds; in fact, the orchestra play the way they always have and always will. The conductor is not allowed to make any sound that you can hear. Some say that the less jerking about he does the better he is. When really at the top of his game a raised eyebrow is said to be enough to indicate surrender. But be sure, it is controlling the applause which is his main function.

The real "primus inter pares" is one of the Principal blowers who begins every concert (the collection of different "pieces" separated by applause) when he makes a sound a bit like a cat and all the others in the orchestra try to get as close to this wail as they can, without actually getting there. This piece is named "Tuning" and probably gets its popularity because it is so short. It does not get a mention in the programme because it is anonymous. Because there is no conductor at this stage no one is expected to applaud this supremo, though it is often considered the best of the pieces. It is certainly so if the concert programme mentions the name "Wagner".

You are allowed to fall asleep (indeed it is expected), but not to snore. Wagner wrote for special loud curly shiny devices in a vain attempt to stop you snoring. People around you will make distinctive noise called "Shushing" and it is polite to point the honour of this out to any of your companions.

Do not try to join in with the orchestra. You are not in their Union.

## Commentary

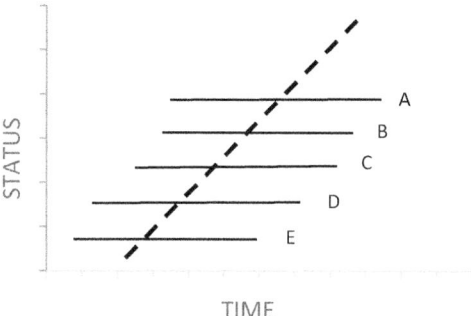

STATUS

TIME

## Employment Plot for the Orchestra

### A=Sawers B= Straight Blowers C= Curly Blowers D= Hitters E=Shouters

Despite the natural envy of each orchestra section of those above them - except for the sawers - no member is allowed to jump up (or down) a rank. Once you are assigned to be a sawer, a straight blower, a curly blower, a hitter or a shouter, then that is your fixed position in the band. Those who claim expertise in more than one section are showoffs and are called amateurs. Everyone thinks they are Competent and everyone else is Incompetent.

The difference between our orchestral personnel and the Angels above is the dimension of time. In the orchestra there is, in theory, if not much in practice, the possibility of rising up the ranks over time. Not so with the Angels.

## 9.5 Solo and Mass Employment Plots

These Organisations are characterised by one Status layer for all - except for one special person who is significantly higher, but no one knows how or why.

<u>Case Study: The Boss</u>

My next-door neighbour has a few chickens (herd? pride? gaggle? Got it – flock) that are really rather pleasant. I can see them from my back-room window and I like to hear their clucking when I am in the garden. They have good and large fox-proof fencing and a nice little dormitory to sleep in at night. Sometimes my neighbour gives me a few eggs which are always nice and brown and taste a lot better than those from the supermarket. She does have a sign outside her house saying "**Free** Range Eggs", but I reckon she charges anybody who calls at her door.

I am sure that the chickens have a pecking order (joke), but it is a mystery to me and, I guess, to my neighbour. Nonetheless, one of the flock stands out. All of them are sort of brownish all over, but she has brightly coloured feathers and a red crown on top of her head. She tends to boss the others around, jabbing at them and insisting on getting to the food first, and she is noticeably bigger than the rest. She is always the first to get up in the morning and insists on waking her sisters with the chicken equivalent of reveille. It seems to me that the remainder of the flock are scared of her. To be frank, I think that she has a bit of an attitude problem. Funnily enough, they all have nice names like Felicity and Daphne, but my neighbour calls her "The Cock".

I am not sure what singles her out from all the other chickens, but I am sure that they all respect her.

Commentary

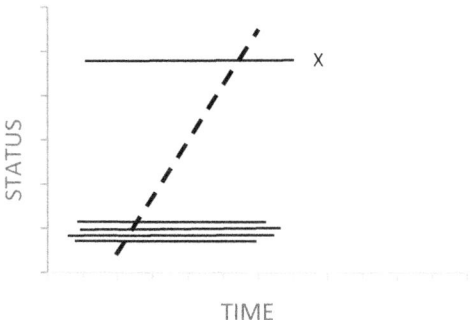

TIME

Employment Plot for the Flock of Chickens

All the chickens bar the special one are on the same level and are thus grouped on the same Career line. The one called "The Cock" obviously is higher in Status (marked with an "X") but it is unclear what Skills, Wealth & Esteem cause this.

We all often ask ourselves "how on earth did he or she get to where they are?" It seems a mystery that a person achieved the position they hold. As with the Cock, that person will have attributes (Skills) that we are unaware of; perspective is all.

Case Study: Monastic Mysteries

Anthony is tired of the Rat Race mainly because he is not very good at it. Having no relatives or even friends to worry about, and being of a religious mind, he decides to become a monk in a small monastery (the monastic order chosen is confidential).

The Abbey personnel constitute just seven other monks and an Abbot.  Anthony soon gets into the swing of things. Now Brother

Anthony enjoys his new life. He is very keen and it seems to him that he out-performs his brothers in all their duties: first up for Matins, last out of Compline, loudest chanter of psalms and hymns, record holder for the sprint around the cloisters, always last in the queue for the bread and gruel and most assiduous in the vegetable gardens and fields.

Brother Anthony's attention turns to the Abbot. What distinguishes him from all the other monks and, in particular, how does one get to be the patriarch? Surely, he himself has all the qualifications due to his enthusiastic spirituality. He has no one to consult (no talking in the ranks!) so his speculations remain internal. In his daily devotions he tries to concentrate on the divine, but his attention keeps wandering back to the Abbot, thinking "What has he got that I have not?" Brother Anthony's prayers on the subject are not answered and he is left to unrequited contemplation in his many lonely hours in his cell.

Commentary

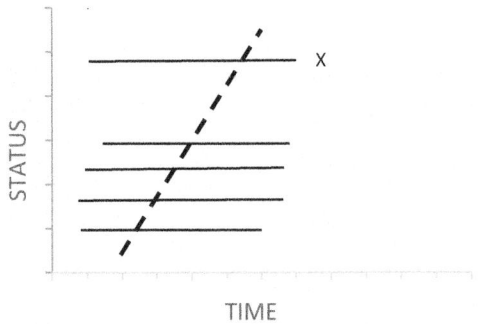

Employment Plot for The Monastery

Again, all the monks have a ranking dependent on their Skills but there is a big difference between them and the Abbot (marked with an X). How the Abbot got to his loftier position is a mystery to

Brother Anthony.  He should remember that God moves in mysterious ways.

Outside of the fraternity, we often meet this type of Employment Plot in businesses where a single person has set up trade and expanded to employ a group of lower-level workers. He owns and runs the establishment, but his staff have little chance of taking his place, even though they may have the necessary Skills.

## 9.6 Employment Plots for Secret Organisations

Little is known about Secret Organisations. They come in two forms: **clandestine** - where members know about some aspects which remain hidden from you and me - and those that, as far as we are told, **do not exist**. We will discuss the former first.

Case Study  The Freemasons

I could not find out anything about this Organisation.

Case Study: In the Closet

Jeremy always fancied his expertise at Hide and Seek since, when he was eight years old, he managed to remain hidden from his siblings for three hours only to emerge to discover that they had forgotten all about him. Early successes in blackmailing his father regarding his relationship with the maid resulted in a sufficiency in lollipops. Spying on his sister in the bath educated him on anatomy. When he learnt to read his chosen milieu was the corpus of Ian Fleming.

On reaching adulthood he was recruited to his country's Secret Service by a secret method. It is possible that his education helped: he went to a secret school and then a secret university where he became fluent in a secret language.

His induction to the furtive guild went like this:

F. "Well done for arriving on time. That means you are immediately promoted from 001 to 002. You are assigned to Group C with the codename W."

W. "Thank you very much. Not far to go to reach 007!"

F. "Don't be silly. That is all a fiction to keep nosey parkers off the scent. A license to kill is only for 784 and above."

W. "I see, I think. How many grades are there?"

F. "Who knows? Not me, certainly."

W. "Could you please give me an outline of my duties in Group C?"

F. "I am in Group D, so I am not permitted to know what Group C does. It is the policy of compartmentalism. Need to know and all that. I expect you will sit at your desk and translate things from (REDACTED) to English. That is what everybody else seems to do. Read, translate, write notes in the margin and sign off WC."

W. "When do I get to operate in the field?"

F. "How do I know. Above my pay grade."

W. "What can I tell my partner I am doing for a living?"

F. "Same as one and all. You work for the Ministry of Culture. The vital thing to remember is that WE DO NOT EXIST."

W. "That's sound all good. Where is the coffee machine?"

F. "If I told you that I would have to shoot you."

Commentary

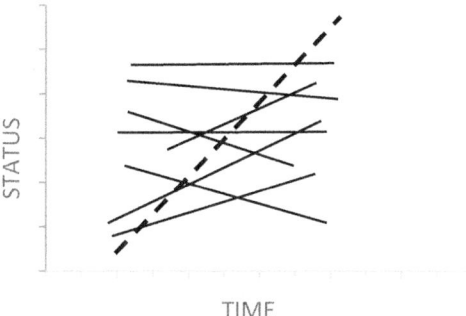

Employment Plot for a Non Existent Organisation

Jeremy is not alone in his inability to assess the Organisation. The whole point is that it is so secret that no one should know what it is. You may think that someone at the top has a clue, but you are mistaken.

Working out who does what in large companies is often as obtuse as this Secret Service; rest assured that nobody else understands either.

This commentary is entirely fictitious. You have not read this. You do not know me and I do not work at the Ministry of Culture. Chew and swallow this chapter.

## 9.7    Employment    Plots    for    Democratic Organisations

Some Organisations claim to be democratic with all participants equal in Status. As you will remember, this is not possible: groups of two or more people must necessarily form a hierarchy. Democratic

Organisations are thus deluded and are a **fallacy**. Two examples are provided to illustrate this misapprehension:

Case Study: The Golden Age

Eleven Knights of the Round Table are gathered in the hall which contains the famous Round Table. The Table is a symbol of equals and is constructed especially so that no one can sit at the head indicating that they are more important than the rest. They await the arrival of King Arthur.

Gawain, "Where did the King sit last time around?"

Percival, "What do you want to know for?"

Gawain, "I just thought I would warm his stool for him."

Percival, "You just want to sit next to him again."

Gawain, "But it is months since I did."

Boris the Younger, "I'll sit here and keep a stool next to me for him."

Percival, "No you don't. You're too young to sit next to the King." Boris the Younger bursts into tears.

Mordred, "He usually sits next to the fire. I'll go there." Merlin suddenly materializes.

Merlin, "Not so fast, Mordred. I forsee that you will be the traitor and must prepare for banishment. You must sit as far from the King as possible."

King Arthur, "Anyone seen Lancelot around?" The Knights shuffle about in embarrassment.

King Arthur, "No matter. I thought that I saw him trying to hide behind an arras (a concealment device later popularized by Polonius in Hamlet, though it did not do him much use)."

The King sits. The Knights scramble to sit nearest to him. There remains a space furthest away from Arthur. He, "Right. To today's business. Any volunteers to seek and find the Holy Grail? It has been a while since we last tried."

All, "Me sir! Please please choose me!"

King Arthur, "How can I choose? Are not we all equal before the Lord and thus equal around this table? I cannot pick from my band of peers. I think that I will send Lancelot. He needs a break."

Commentary

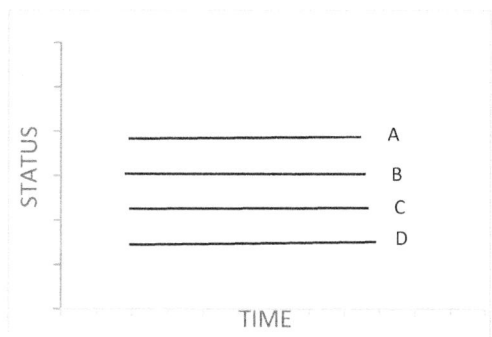

Employment Plot for Knights of the Round Table

They are, of course, all mistaken in their understanding of equality. There is a clear grading: from the bottom up D = Boris the Younger, then nine knights (C) about the same, then B = King Arthur and, at the top, A = Lancelot.

Always be cynical when someone claims to run a democratic organization. This is a "contradiction in terms", a description that will be recognized by the logicians amongst us. To the rest of us it means "No way, Jose".

Case Study: The Collective

Jacob and Abigail are members of an agricultural Kibbutz. They are the parents of Rebecca, their seven-year-old daughter whom they see and play with in Rebecca's Children's House for the permitted two hours every afternoon. They are encouraged at these times to play with the other children in her age group too, so that Rebecca does not come to think that she is the personal possession of Jacob and Abigail but belongs to all the Kibbutzniks.

Their collective is an orthodox cooperative. Everything is shared. Jacob and Abigail eat in the communal dining hall, but not together as this might suggest a relationship. Abigail, as a woman, is equal in all respects to the men and does as much labour in the fields as them. She and Jacob are given their daily tasks from the Duty Sheets posted by the elected leaders.

There are some in the Kibbutz who are known to not pull their weight; they are viewed as parasites and some sulking goes on.

Jacob and Abigail are happy in their chosen way of life and Rebecca seems to be content.

Commentary

Employment Plot for The Kibbutz

The idea of the Kibbutz is Utopian, a blend of socialism and Zionism where deliberate efforts are made for members to be equal, particularly between the genders and the children. Of course they are not. Putting aside the elected leaders and the children, hierarchies are bound to form amongst the rest of the Kibbutzniks. The experiment in living (which is what it is) deserves a chance of success but social parity will not be a part if it; that is against human nature.

You may well want to join a kibbutz for many reasons (some not wholesome) but please do so with your eyes open. You will start at an uncomfortable bottom.Can Organisation plots be used to make League Tables? Yes, they can if everyone in the table is dead - otherwise you do not know how Career plots will finish. Comparison of different Careers with each other on the same plot should be regarded as a theoretical exception, but here are our two specimens anyway.

Case Study: When in Rome

The year is 1500 and three Italian chums are chewing the fat over their vino da tavola and are arguing over who is the greatest of the current painters.

Giovani, "My vote goes to Michelangelo. What he does on his back is sensational."

Marco, "How can you tell? That ceiling is so far away all his mistakes could be smothered over and nobody could tell." Big booboo with the fingers not meeting, though.

Giovanni, "You can get close to his Last Judgment. No slipups there!"

Luigi, "One swallow does not a summer make. Your Michelangelo spends too much time chipping the block and fawning on the Pope to paint enough for me. I go for Leonardo. Sure, he also spends too much time on his military stuff and scientific whatnots but when he does produce they are the best. No one comes anywhere near his sfumato."

Marco, "Sfumato, tomato. That one with the lady with the funny look reminds me of my mistress's smirk when I take my clothes off. I go for chiascuro and that means Raphael."

Luigi, "It's all right for you two. You can get into the Vatican Palace any time you want to gorge yourselves on your Michelangelos and your Raphaels. Us common folk have to make do with what we can get a moniker on. You and your "High Renaissance". My kind has to make do with the Low stuff."

Marco, "Can we at least agree to exclude Michelangelo as he is very much work in progress?"

Giovanni, "Not on your life. I agree that his sculptures will not pass the test of time and they will soon be forgotten but we are talking about his paintings and drawings here."

Luigi, "Oh, so we are including drawings now, are we? That puts my Leonardo way, way above your daubers."

And so on. . .

Commentary

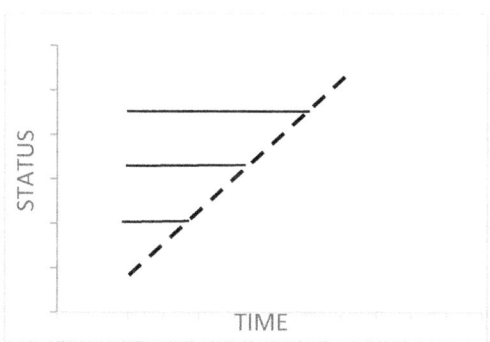

Employment Plot for Three Renaissance Painters

It goes without saying that all three of our painters are Competent throughout their lives. The Career Path lengths describe the span of their lives. In the argument as to who is the best, you guess who is whom.

Comparing the Skills of different people misses the point; be they artists, footballers, authors or whatever, the important thing is that they bring their Skills to their profession to be appreciated, not compared.

Case Study: Chamber of Horrors

Four of the Great British Serial Killers are Harold Shipman, Denis Nilsen, Fred West (plus spouse) and John Christie (serial killers who were Great British, not that they were British and Great).

Since they are all dead it is possible to produce a league table on an Employment plot. Shipman killed 265+, Nilsen 15, West 12+ and Christie 8+.

Commentary

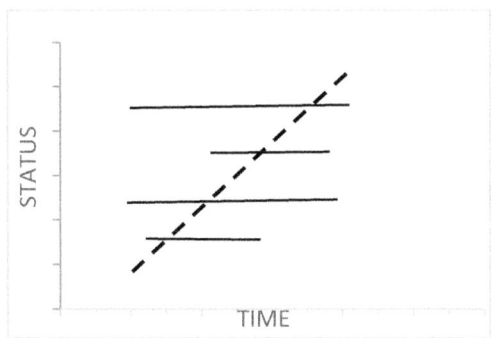

Employment Plot for GB Serial Killers

This plot is a reminder that Status does not have a moral compass. If you can accept that the number killed reflects Skills and infamy reflects Esteem, then an Employment plot is viable. The order of Status is taken as the number killed and the ZSP points designate how long each murderer "practised" before discovery.

Not all Careers or Occupations are praiseworthy but that does not stop them being described in Employment Plots.

## 9.8 Conclusions and Chapter's Key Points

Thus ends the description of the Employment Plot model. Hopefully with this Chapter on Irregular plots you will have a broad overview of the model and its potential to analyse  how Careers and Organisations can intertwine.

**There are many Employment Plots that are Irregular**

**Organisations that form Irregular Plots are best avoided**

**They are not a reliable route to increased Status**

# CHAPTER 10 THE PETER PRINCIPLE EXAMINED

## 10.1. Introduction

In the introductory chapter 1, I suggested that my General Theory of Employment Plots should be applicable to all types of Occupations in all types of Organisation.

I also proposed that, in common with dear old Albert, a General Theory should reinterpret any Special Theory that went before it. I have delegated the Peter Principle as my Special Theory and this chapter examines it in light of my Employment Plots. You may well ask why I have chosen the Peter Principle from all the possible management theories? The answer is that:

it is probably the best known and is memorable.

it is the prettiest.

There is no mass of research papers published on it,          reducing the need for extensive study on my (and your) part.

It has a long track record.

Most importantly, it is succinct.

## 10.2 The Peter Principle Once More

A reminder: the Peter Principle is:

*"In a Hierarchy every Employee Tends to Rise to*

*His level of Incompetence."*

You will recall that I was puzzled about three things with the Principle

(1) How come nobody thinks that the Principle applies to them?

(2) We all know at least someone who is incompetent and yet is promoted.

(3) We all know someone (fewer) who survive their careers without a blemish.

It is now time to address those puzzles using Employment Plots as my analytical tool.

## 10.3  Puzzle Number 1

"How come nobody thinks that the Principle applies to them?"

This one is easily dealt with: it is all a question of perspective. Section 2.6 above described how no perspective of Status is a right one. In particular, you own view of your Status will be different and usually superior to that of any pesky Peter Principle aficionados. This raises an important question about the Principle: just who is it that decides whether someone is Competent or Incompetent?

## 10.4 Puzzle Number 2

"We all know at least someone who is incompetent and yet continues to be promoted."

This one is a bit more complicated. According to Dr. Peter's work, his Principle applies to hierarchies. Therefore, in any representative Employment Plot the Occupation Tracks must be Inclined, as Level and Declining Occupation Tracks are not hierarchical.

Similarly, the Career Paths must be Inclined, as the candidate gets promoted. In addition, that Career Line must cross the Occupation line, as the candidate, under the Principle, moves from Competent to Incompetent. This can all be represented in a theoretical Employment Plot:

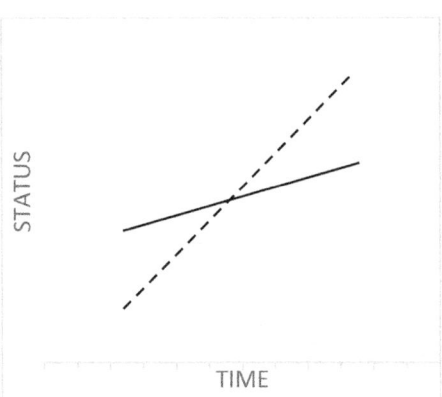

Theoretical Employment Plot for the Peter Principle

This Plot is what my General Theory describes but Dr. Peter has it differently:

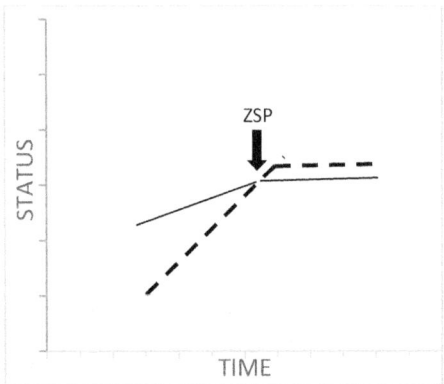

Employment Plot According to the Peter Principle

Our individual's Career Line rises, with Skills above equivalent (time-wise) Wealth and Esteem on the Occupation Line until it reaches **just past** what I have designated as the Zero Sum Point (ZSP). It is there that our subject reaches his or her level of Incompetence and, according to Dr. Peter's work, remains at that level for the rest of their career. Meanwhile the Occupation Track would continue on its normal trajectory for those more fortunate.

To help us resolve this disagreement I call on another Case Study:

Case Study:  A Battle Royal

The year is 1066. An English King called Harold is relaxing in his tent one night near the seaside at Hastings. His is reading a pamphlet on Greek philosophers and studies the Zeno paradox, which both intrigues him and massively boosts his self-confidence. He summons a messenger and sends him over to call on William (not yet Conqueror) and ask if he fancies a battle the next day. William replies "Sounds good, shall we say 10 for 10.30 with a break for lunch at about 2 if things are going well?"

The battle commences promptly. Things are going pretty good for Harold when he sees a Norman archer fire off an arrow. Harold says to himself, "that arrow is heading straight for me. I reckon it is about 128 yards away (England had not gone metric in 1066). It is a good thing that I understand now from Zeno that the arrow is halfway towards hitting me. When it is 64 yards away it will still be only three quarters towards me and then three eighths and then three sixteenths and so on ad infinitum so can never reach me. I am safe due to the brilliance of Zeno".

The arrow penetrates Harold's eye, the battle was lost, French became the language of the hoity-toity in England and the teaching of Greek philosophy was only allowed in private schools.

Commentary Zeno's paradox and its unfortunate effect on our misguided King centres on the difference between an infinite series and reality. If you take a series of **levels** in sequence you get to a single point. This, I think, is what happens in the Peter Principle. By moving up the Occupation ladder, which is defined by distinct stages (e.g. Assistant, Manager, Senior etc), you arrive at the ZSP, beyond which you can go no further. But the fact is that the arrow **did** go through poor Harold's eye and people **can** and **do** get promoted beyond their ZSP. Just look around your office.

Although Occupation Tracks are usually marked by discrete stages, the Career Paths are continuous; you do not wake up one morning to find yourself transformed from junior cygnet to a senior swan. You gain Skills incrementally day by day.

Dr. Peter's work investigates in some depth his concept of the "Final Placement Syndrome" and also speculates that, in theory at least, an organization fully subject to the Peter Principle will reach a state of stasis where everyone is **just** at their level of Incompetence (i.e. just past their ZSP). Looking around several government departments will easily demonstrate that these Organisations employ many personnel in that state.

My issue with the Peter Principle is not that people rise to their level of Incompetence, but whether or not they **then** make progress in their careers. Dr. Peter's view is that people remain at their Final Place as soon as they are Incompetent; to me it seems common sense that a person's Skills should have the chance to continue to improve after they become Incompetent.

Dr. Peter's hierarchy is typified by occupations and careers marked, by **distinct stages** (Assistant, Senior etc.) Employment Plots show a smooth progress like an arrow in the air.

I am sorry to say this, but I disagree with the Peter Principle in this respect: Dr Peter appears to assume that "everybody" has but one level of Competence throughout their careers, whereas I believe that "everybody" can and does improve their Skills from the beginning to the end of their working life.

## 10.5  ZSPs

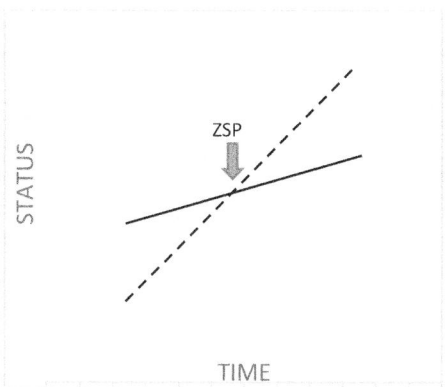

<u>Model Employment Plot Highlighting the ZSP</u>

The Zero Sum Point (ZSP) is a **critical point** in Career Progression. Skills have increased and are now in balance with the Wealth and Esteem provided. All is harmonious and fair and just. It is at this point in your career progress when you think that you have "hit a brick wall".  But business does not recognize the terms "fair" and "just". There is **no reason** why you cannot continue to increase your Skills and continue up the ladder. The idea of a "brick wall" in your career is a myth perpetrated by **you**. If you believe in natural justice, that Wealth and Esteem are best balanced with Skills, then you will not get over that wall and you will be in the minority. You deserve better than that.

In this classic hierarchical employment situation the Occupation Track is **steeper** than the Career Path. What this essentially means is that it is longer and that means more possibilities. It also means that, if you get past your ZSP, the Wealth & Esteem increases **by a multiple** as you claw your way up.

Have you ever wondered how the so-called "Captains of Industry" earn such ridiculous salaries? The classic Employment Plot above demonstrates that the higher you are the bigger the ratio between rewards and abilities.

## 10.6  How Over Appreciated People Get Promoted

I guess I need to explain further how over-appreciated people get promoted up the ladder.

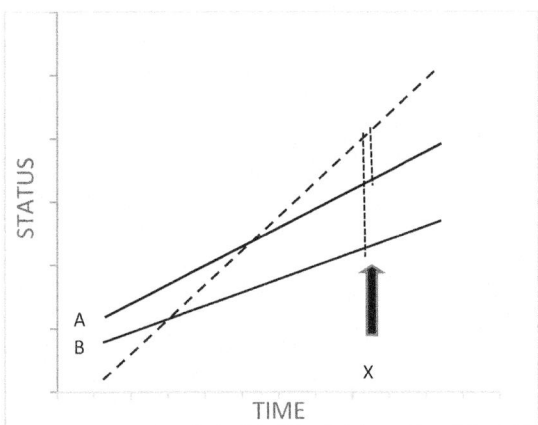

Two Inclined Career Lines Plotted Against an Inclined Organisation Track

In the above plot two candidates A and B work in the same Occupation in an Organisation. A has a higher starting point in their Career and a steeper slope than B. At a time X they are both considered for a new role in the Organisation. Both are Incompetent, but A **is less Incompetent than B** and gets the job. What matters is **relative** Status, there is no absolute grade of Competency. To reinforce this: **no one is actually Competent or Incompetent, but they can be seen as either.**

What also matters is **who** makes the decision on that promotion. He or she is likely to be further up the Occupation ladder and therefore probably even more Incompetent than the two candidates, but it is his or her perspective on the Skills of the candidates that will count. The perspectives of colleagues (whose voices on Competence /Incompetence are likely to be those broadcasting the evidence of the Peter Principle), matter little. As we have discovered, the candidates themselves will not regards themselves as Incompetent.

This is to repeat what we learnt from Chapter 2 on Status: there is no absolute value of Status but only one compared to another. To climb up the ladder you must only (!) be better than the competition, not have some generalized and amorphous set of Skills.

## 10.7  Looking Up and Down

As you observe those fortunate ones above you in the Organisation you will notice that they are likely either less Competent or more Incompetent than you and the gap between their rewards (Wealth and Esteem) and their Skills is greater than yours.

The fact is that usually the higher up the Occupation Track then the difficulty in performing a role is exponentially greater. If it was normal for the higher-ups to be over-compensated then the market would have dealt with it.

Looking down your Occupation Track and by thinking in terms of Employment plots two other things stand out: Firstly, when your boss tries to do your job for you because they are comfortable being back where they were relatively Competent, don't let them, shoo them off.

Secondly, **Personnel beneath you are better at their jobs than you are at yours.** Obviously you could do their job better than they do –

that is why you were promoted. But you are paid and valued to do **your** job, not theirs.

## 10.8  Puzzle Number 3

"We all know someone (fewer) who survive their careers without a blemish."

The fact is that we all can think of at least one person who is Competent throughout their career. Take your pick from Mother Theresa, James Bond, your childhood pet rabbit, Ella Fitzgerald, your history teacher, an author of management books, your mother ... If all else fails just look in the mirror. For me, Chapter 4's duo of Nelson Mandela and Father Christmas will suffice.

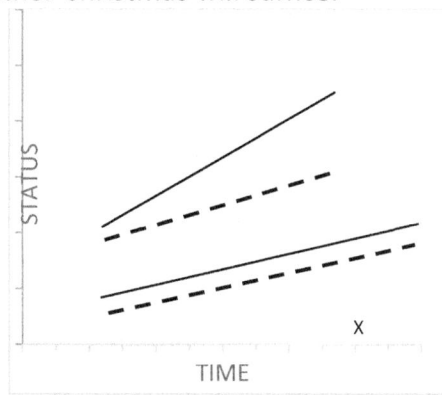

Example Employment Plots for the Permanently Competents

Dr. Peter's work denies this and stipulates that, first of all, a person is promoted until they reach the ZSP and then he or she settles into what is described as "The Final Placement" with its consequent "Syndrome".

The first argument to be made is that there is confusion as to what Dr. Peter's work actually says. In the text (and what I take to be the authority) it is:

*"In a Hierarchy every Employee **Tends to Rise** to*

*His level of Incompetence."*

But on the blurb on the back of my paperback copy it is given as:

*"In a Hierarchy every Employee **Rises** to*

*His level of Incompetence."*

This false description pops up in much of the literature about the Principle. Indeed, if you ask someone what he understands to be the Peter Principle they usually will give you the second (false) definition.

Detailed reading of Dr. Peter's work does not help: Hull sometimes postulates the universality of Incompetence but elsewhere admits that there are exceptions. In the body of Dr. Peter's work a significant small section is:

"So, given enough time – and assuming the existence of enough ranks in the hierarchy – each employee rises to, and remains at, his level of incompetence."

Peter's Corollary states:

*"In time, every post **tends** (my emphasis) to be occupied by an employee who is incompetent to carry out its duties."* (Dr. Peter's italics)

When Dr. Peter uses the verb **tends** I take it to mean that not all employees rise to Incompetence and that the common appreciation of his Principle goes beyond his original intentions. In short, people can and do remain Competent throughout their Careers.

To reinforce the argument, Dr. Peter's work also devotes a chapter to outlining five common illusory exceptions to the Principle, which may be seen as labouring the point.

## 10.9   Conclusions and Chapter Key Points

In scientific terms, a General Theory broadening a Special Theory is allowed to go back and correct things in its erstwhile publication; in fact it is considered very clever to do so if the same author writes both.

For me the General Theory postulates Employment Plots for **all** types of Occupations in all types of Organisation and should consider the Special Theory (the Peter Principle) applicable to hierarchical organisations only.

Dr. Peter thinks that **all** employees **tend** to reach their level of incompetence and **stay there**. I think that all employees **can** get to their level of incompetence but can then continue to increase their Skills and be promoted to higher levels of Wealth and Esteem.

**Differences in Perspectives explain why very few people think that they are Incompetent**

**Employment Plots contradict the Peter Principle in their ideas of Career Progress beyond the ZSP (or level of Incompetence)**

**The often false re-statement of the Peter Principle ("rises" rather than "tends to rise") is perhaps the reason why some people appear always Competent**

# CHAPTER 11  CAREER ANALYSIS and PLANNING

## 11.1  Introduction

From the first sentences of this book, you will remember that the idea of Employment Plots is to act as a kind of microscope allowing the magnification of, and focusing on, employment situations via a simple visual device.

Any theory, even one as elegant as Employment Plots, will gain considerable kudos if it can be shown to have practical application. This final chapter provides a few examples from the different stages of a normal career to illustrate some simple career situations. Of course, the decisions we face in our working lives are generally more complex than my examples, but I trust the instances below will give an idea of the applicability of Employment Plots to career analysis and planning. You will criticise these examples as being simply common sense; firstly I will be delighted if they conform to reality and secondly "common sense" is only obvious when it is evident.

I have chosen my examples from the stages through which a "normal" career might develop. Therefore the demonstration Employment Plots all have Inclined Career Paths and Inclined Occupation Tracks.

Of course, I have spent much time in writing (and, if you have got this far, you have made much effort in reading) about other types of Organisation and their associated Occupation Tracks. The starting point for drawing your own Employment Plot is to decide what type of Organisation you are employed in and which Occupation Tracks it offers. All the Regular and Irregular Organisations discussed in previous chapters can be analysed with the techniques that follow.

## 11.2  Going to University?

(Or any other form of tertiary education; I have taken university as my example).

Many youngsters (God how I envy them) have to make a choice career-wise as to whether or not to study beyond school, always assuming that they have done well enough at that school to be in a position to make that choice.

Case Study:  The Four Amigos

Alan, Beth and Colin have just completed their final school exams, each with radiant success. They all enroll to study Physics at university. Their friend Douglas has not done so well and he decides to go straight from school to a job at Engineering Corp.

## Commentary

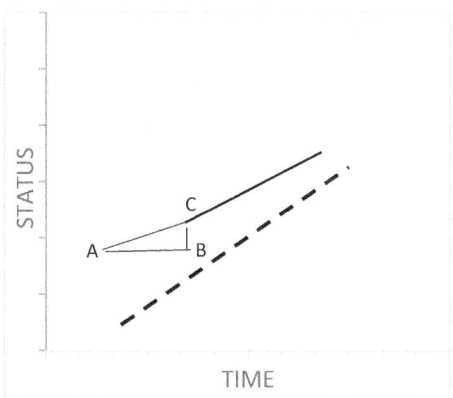

### Employment Scenarios for Alan, Beth and Colin and Douglas

Our three university students start their courses at A in the above Plot and graduate at B. You will see that none of the three have improved their Skills in the time between A and B; this is because we are observing from the point of view of potential employers (designated by the Occupation Track), and they assume that students learn nothing unless graced with a degree certificate. Consequently, when the three university students graduate their Skills level magically jump from B to C.

Alan wants to be a lecturer in Physics:

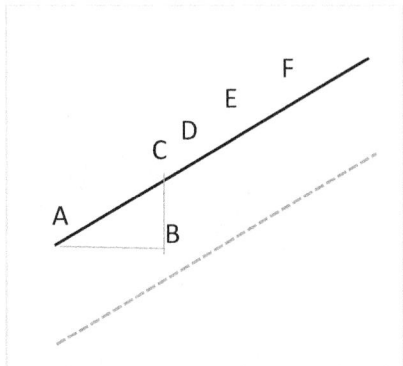

<u>Employment Plot for Alan</u>

To achieve his aim he must do a doctorate as a minimum so he stays at university (C to D), qualifies, works as a post-doc (E) achieves his goal and joins his Occupation Track (University Staff) at F. Note that he joins that Occupation Plot at its lowest level of Wealth & Esteem; importantly he cannot join that Track **unless** he goes to university and studies further for his doctorate and indeed post-doc. The choice to go or not is made for him if he wishes to pursue his chosen career.

Beth wants to work for Engineering Corp (where Douglas has just joined):

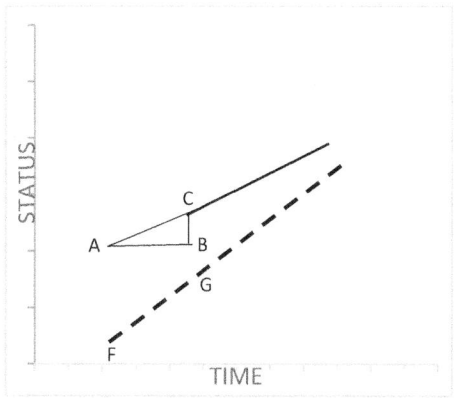

Employment Plot for Beth and Douglas

She completes her degree (A to B) and qualifies and thus improves her Skills to C. This allows her to join Engineering Corp (the Occupation line) at G, which is above its first initial recruit level. Meanwhile Douglas has no degree and has embarked on his Engineering Corp Career at F. He has put in the same time (A to B or F to G) and earns the same Wealth & Esteem as Beth.

Dr. Peter's work is of the opinion that there is not much to be gained between Beth's and Douglas's route to success and I see no reason to disagree with him. Going to university is **not necessary** to joining some Occupation Tracks.

Meanwhile Colin graduates and chooses to begin working life at the bottom of a small hotel group that does not have a graduate training programme:

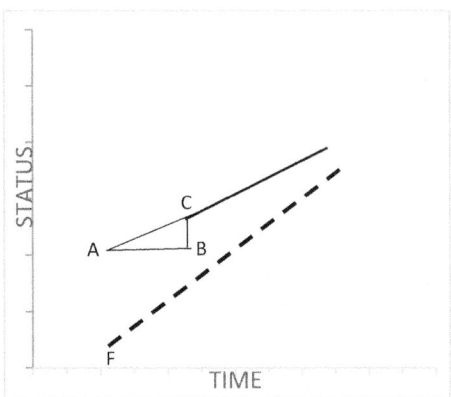

Employment Plot for Colin

Colin joins his hotel group at F, wasting, at first sight, the time spent at university (A to B). In his case his investment in his degree is only marginally **relevant** to his career.

The Employment Plots show that choosing your Career first, before taking the decision to go to university or not, is wise.

"If you don't know where you want to go then it doesn't matter which path you take." (The Cheshire Cat to Alice in Lewis Carroll's "Alice in Wonderland")

You will say (and you will be correct) that this is pretty obvious; indeed it is, especially when you look at it with the focused eye of the Employment Plot. Yet this is not apparent to many. Going to university often becomes an end in itself, frequently encouraged by parents or other influencers.

I would like to add something to all of the above, namely what happens to **Life Skills** when going to university. Most people who do so claim that the Life Skills gained there are as important as Work Skills. For all our four students, that gain in Life Skills and Status is earnt irrespective of which Occupation Track they join.

## 11.3 Choosing Your Occupation: Skills

Choosing your occupation may seem to be a luxury to many and indeed it is; getting a job in the first place is an achievement. Presuming that you have a chance to influence that initial selection, or to choose another Occupation later in life, then two attributes are relevant: Skills, and attitude to risk. To begin with Skills, I presume that you wish to maximize your Wealth & Esteem over your working life. This means choosing a planned Career Path that fits best with an Occupation Track with high Wealth & Esteem potential. Matching Career Paths and Occupation Tracks on your Employment Plots is an essential requisite to achieving that desired Wealth & Esteem. Your Skills play two roles in that Employment Plot. Firstly, the quantity and quality of your **applicable** Skills will assist in achieving **a high start point** and a **steeper slope** on your Career Path. "Applicable" is the key glue that binds Career Paths to Occupation Tracks.

I recommend that you undertake an audit of various perspectives of your Skills. Naturally the most important perspective will be your own but seeking the views of others will help. Professional careers advice is urged. You can then look to ways to increase existing Skills and learn new ones applicable to a chosen Occupation Track.

Initial Skills are your starting assets; progress is driven by the **desire** to march up the ladder and this aspiration is more important. You may start with all the apparent Skills to be a doctor, an accountant or a chef but if you want to be a racing driver, despite being myopic and nervy (starting point of your Career Path), then that choice could be more important in the end (or perhaps not).

Again, the balance between Work and Life Statuses should be considered; remember that the aim is to maximize Total Status.

## 11.4 Choosing your Career: Attitudes to Risk

As well as a survey of your Skills, I suggest that you review your **Attitudes to Risk** alongside all the other factors in this book: are there promotion opportunities where you are, is it a hierarchical or level organisation etc. Attitudes to Risk is a familiar concept in financial circles but should, I propose, also be considered in choosing your initial Career Path.

### Ambition

Case Study : Bewigged or not Bewigged

Emily has taken her first degree and the required post graduate qualifications to enter the legal profession. Which Career Path to take?

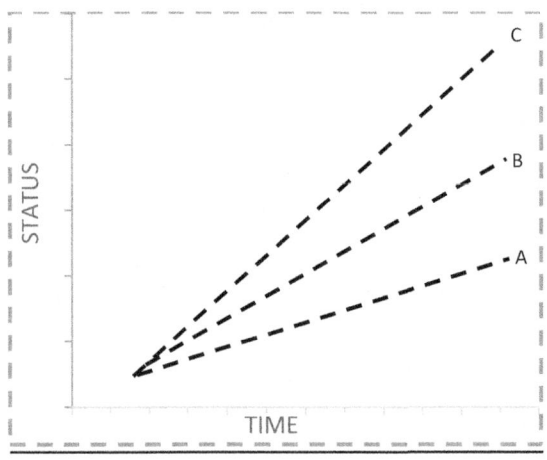

Possible Occupation Paths in the Legal World

This figure represents three possible Occupation Tracks in the Organisation of the legal world. "A" represents the Track for a solicitor, "B" the Track for a commercial lawyer and "C" that of a barrister. Of course, those acquainted with the actual legal universe will vehemently argue that this model bears no relationship to their actual profession, but if they have already accepted Superman and the Tooth Fairy then I am sure that they will suspend their critical faculties for just this one Case Study.

You will observe that the three Occupation Tracks have different slopes and final levels of Wealth & Esteem. Which Track should Emily choose at the start of her Career?

She is, of course, ambitious for Wealth & Esteem (are not we all?) but there are other considerations. She does not like conflict, she is not (yet) the best public speaker, she has little experience of the commercial world and is vaguely aware of a maternal instinct which will, at some time in the future, need to be satisfied.

Emily needs to honestly measure her own **Attitude to Risk**: to choose to be a solicitor (A) involves the smallest slope which will have the lowest competition. At the other end of the scale choosing to be a barrister (C) offers the prospect of the highest rewards, but the necessary Skills demanded are also the highest. Let us use Employment Plots to illustrate these two situations (choosing to be a commercial lawyer (B) comes in between).

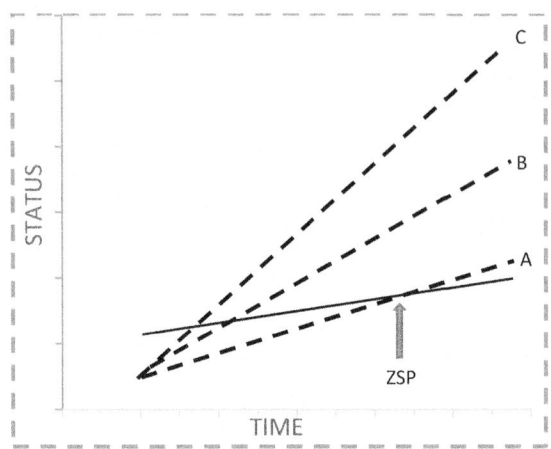

**Employment Plot for Emily (Low Risk Option)**

<u>Commentary</u>    The above Employment Plot shows Emily's Employment Plot if she has a low Attitude to Risk. In any forecasting of your Employment Plot it seems sensible and conservative to plan to reach your ZSP (Skills offered equate to Wealth & Esteem provided) but to go no further. In this Low Risk preference Emily would do best choosing to be a solicitor since this Occupation Track (A) would deliver, at the end of promotion (the ZSP Point), the highest level of Wealth and Esteem i.e. higher than the ZSP points on the other two Occupation tracks B and C.

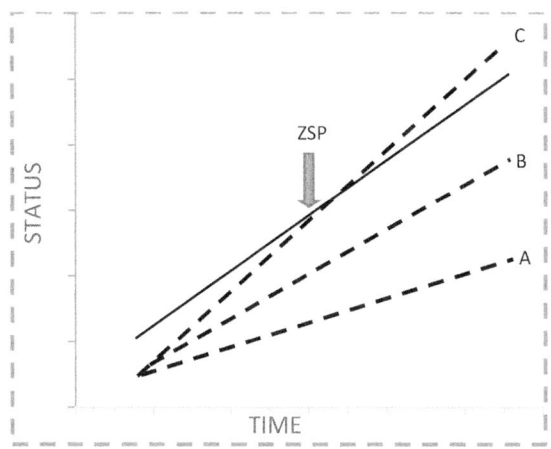

Employment Plot for Emily (High Risk Option)

The figure shows Emily's Employment Plot if she has a high Attitude to Risk. In this case she should choose to be a barrister, since this delivers the highest Wealth & Esteem at a higher ZSP. If she has decided to be a solicitor with this Attitude to Risk she would never have achieved her potential, with Skills always above Wealth & Esteem. As a generalisation, risk is proportional to **specialization**: the more specialized your chosen career the higher will be your rewards, but that will involve higher risk with resultant difficulty in getting another job should you be unfortunate enough to lose an existing one. There are a lot more solicitors than barristers.

It is, of course, very hard to engage in self-analysis so early in your career; friends and family will be only too happy to assist you.

**Private Versus Public**

Two general Organisation/Occupation Tracks need possible consideration in choosing your first job. The first of these is the choice between the private and public sectors:

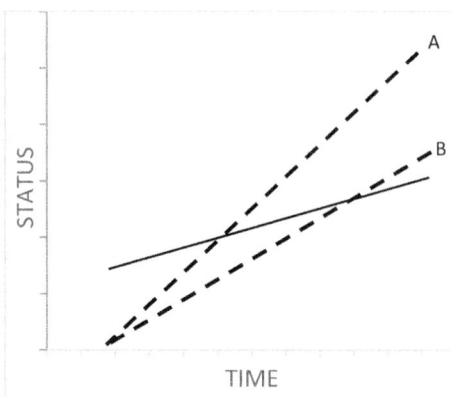

<u>Model Employment Plots for (A) Private and (B) Public Occupation Tracks</u>

The above Employment Plot suggests that Occupations in the Private Sector are more "risky" than those in the Public sector and thus more highly rewarded. Whether or not this is true is up to you to decide.

**Function Versus Service**

The occupations in most commercial organisations can be divided between **Functions,** where the role is to be actively involved in the business, and **Services,** which are there to support those functions:

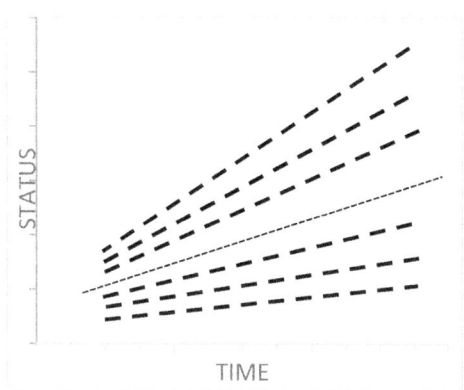

Occupation Tracks Divided by Functions and Services

In the above Employment Plot (and as a very wide generalization) occupations that are actually involved in the production of the enterprise will have higher Wealth & Esteem than those that are there to support those functions.

As an example I choose a large retail clothing company: the professions there will usually have a pecking order as follows: from the top: Buying, Merchandising, Store Management in the "doing" category, followed by Systems, Marketing, Finance and HR in the "service" category. As well as having higher Wealth & Esteem, the "doing" personnel are more likely to achieve senior positions in the company.

In recompense, those in the "service" functions have more transferability – their Skills can be applied in companies not specializing in retail clothing.

## Attitudes to Wealth and Esteem

In much of this book the implication has been that Wealth and Esteem are closely related; indeed much of the time they have been lumped together as "Wealth & Esteem". This is generally the case when both are driven by high levels of Skills. At the outset of your

Career, when Skills are yet to be realised, it is worth considering your attitude to them both because you may feel that one would have priority over the other if it were to come to a choice. High Wealth (e.g. that earned by a "liver off immoral earnings" aka a pimp) comes with low Esteem. High Esteem (e.g. a nurse) does not generally procure high Wealth. As you start out in your working life you should ponder your priorities.

## 11.5 Climbing the Ladder

The Case Study for this section is the most interesting of all: YOU! I suspect that you are on a Career Path and thereby Occupation Track in an Organisation and you are concerned about your progress up the ladder.

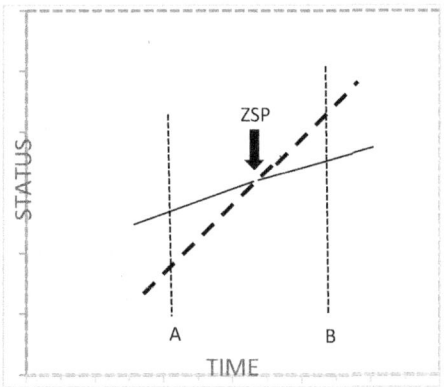

Your Potential Employment Plot

Here you are, having started your Career at point A in time and now considering a rise to point B; there are other "possible" levels on the Occupation Track higher than this, but you are being realistic and "know your place". Naturally, you are anxious as to how quickly you can get to point B. Factors to consider will include:

Chance: Plan and plot as much as you like, I will wager that the biggest influence on your career is luck. There is no way you can strategise for this. Most importantly, do not look back on decisions you have made in the past, thinking that things would have been better had you not made that decision. You cannot possibly imagine the future of any such choice – you could have fallen under a bus.

Who You Know: Will usually be the second biggest factor in your Career progression; cultivate one and all.

Skills: The Employment Plot shows the relationship between Wealth & Esteem rewarded for Skills provided. To climb the ladder you must show that you are able to **deliver on the necessary Skills**. The normal way to do this, as we have seen, is to show Competence at your current level, but you should take any opportunity to demonstrate your abilities at a higher level should the opportunity arise. **Progress is dependent on applicable Skills.** You must think of your Skills narrowly to concentrate on applicability, but also broadly to utilise talents underneath the radar e.g., having a compromising photo of your boss at the last Christmas party, or marrying the boss's daughter.

Comparability: Remember, whatever your Skills in the abstract, their value lies in how they compare with those of your competitors. It is worth drawing the Employment Plots of those nasty impediments to analyse the opposition.

Promotion usually occurs internally i.e., to those already in the Organisation - though not necessarily from those on your own Occupation Track. This is the natural order of things and you should understand your place in the system. However, there are three common exceptions to this rule, and you should be aware of the implications. Firstly, an external candidate is appointed above you. This is unnatural: businesses usually prefer to appoint/promote internally. It is cheaper and less risky (better the devil you know etc.) and encourages all employees in the belief that they too can advance in the company. Since an external appointment is exceptional, if it does happen the important thing to understand is that this reflects badly on you personally. You need to take stock.

Secondly, someone in your company is shifted sideways to a role above you. This only happens when the said individual has shown Incompetence in his or her previous job and, because of the Ratchet Effect (as discussed in Chapter 4), cannot be demoted. For once you must indulge in teamwork with your peers. This character has demonstrated his or her Incompetence; sustained undermining of him or her will get them moved on again.

Thirdly, and very rarely, is the circumstance where someone is demoted to the level above you, despite the Ratchet Effect. You need to take great care; the person thus relegated probably has the Skills to operate at their new level and will have made "friends" at his or her old level. Sustained undermining, either individually or through teamwork, is likely to be a dangerous tactic. Better to try to earn brownie points with the poor soul so that, when he or she is moved on or out (which is bound to happen) you will be numero uno to succeed.

Case Study:  Animal House

A company called Perfect Pet Foods is owned by a lady called Mrs. Elephant who creates a new position of Sales Manager reporting to her. This lucky animal will take over the responsibility of managing the sales team. Mrs. Elephant makes it known that anyone in the sales team is welcome to apply for the new role.

There are only two guys in the frame, a Mr. Tortoise and a Mr. Hare. Mr. Hare has only just joined the company and is a bit flash. Mr.

Tortoise has been there for some time and is more staid. Mrs. Elephant is hoping for both flash and staid, as she herself is exactly that, and she wants someone in her own image.

Mr. Tortoise is already in with Mrs. Elephant's secretary, a Miss Python, which is definitely a plus. Mr. Hare, however, works hard on this (chocolates, flowers etc). He is disconcerted to find that, by the time he achieves sufficient familiarity with Miss Python, Mr. Tortoise has now been awarded a Sales Diploma through studying at night school. Mr. Hare hurries to buy a Sales Diploma from a college in India, which he ostentatiously hangs on the wall above his desk in the office.

Mr. Hare is most irritated to discover that, while he was waiting for his Diploma to arrive from India, Mr. Tortoise had learnt Excel (from the same night school so at a discounted rate) and could now put all of his clients and appointments onto a spreadsheet. Working through the nights, Mr. Hare does his best to clue up on computer programmes, not having the option of attending the night school as he was expelled; another story.

Mr. Hare and Mr. Tortoise both come in for the final interview neck and neck.

Mrs. Elephant cannot make up her mind as to which of the two candidates is the better, thinking that both of them are just a little shy of the qualities she needs. So she employs a recruitment agency to bring in someone from outside to fill the role of Sales Manager. Mr. Gorilla has exactly the right blend of solidity and power required, an excellent CV showing a good track record of managing family groups of salespeople and is a vegetarian. He is appointed as Sales Manager, much to the displeasure of Mr. Tortoise and Mr. Hare.

However, after a few months, rumours begin to spread concerning Mr. Gorilla and Miss Python. Then comes the occasion when the lissom serpent is discovered in flagrante wrapped around the neck of Mr. Gorilla and giving him gentle squeezes. He is required to leave the company "to spend more time with his large family". Mrs. Elephant has learnt her lesson with recruitment agencies and regrets a failure to get a rebate on her fees. Mr. Hare is then promoted to Sales Manager.

Commentary

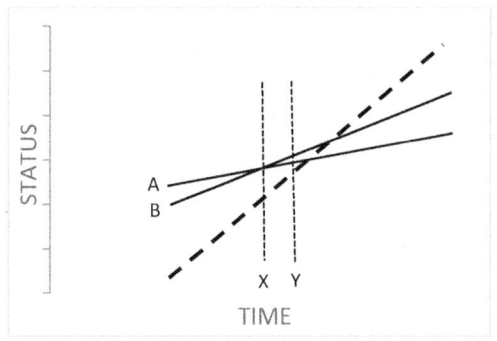

Employment Plots for Mr. Hare and Mr. Tortoise

At the time of the interviews (X) Mr. Tortoise (A) and Mr. Hare (B) are neck and neck but Mrs. Elephant does not think that they are up to the new job of Sales Manager. Mr. Hare continues to increase his Skills at a faster rate than Mr. Tortoise so that, when Mr. Gorilla leaves the company (time Y), he is ahead of Mr. Tortoise and gets the job. Note that, at this time Y neither of the two candidates have reached their ZSPs.

You naturally regard your colleagues as the main competitors for promotion; keep an eye out for job advertisements or other signs of your company looking beyond their walls!

Rate of Ascent: Of course, you are unhappy with the rate at which you are progressing in your company and climbing the ladder. The first thing to understand is that the rate of advancement diminishes as you go up the ladder.

Simply put, the further up the Organisation Track, the harder it is to take the next step. If you are below your ZSP there will be a "push" up the ladder due to the imbalance of Wealth & Esteem versus Skills (Wealth & Esteem < Skills) and this will seem unfair. Similarly, if and when you pass your ZSP, there will be a drag or "pull" on progress (Wealth & Esteem > Skills.) That is why passing your ZSP is so difficult; difficult but not impossible.

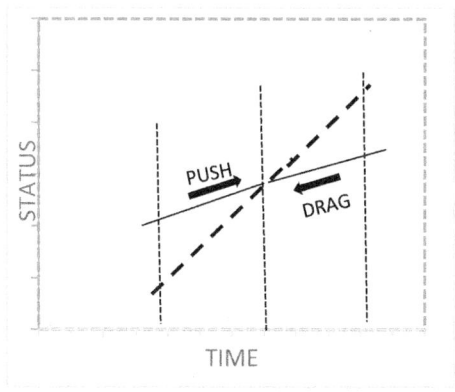

Dynamics of Rates of Promotion

Proportionally, the further you are from your ZSP the stronger the push/pull effect is, reflecting the quantitative difference between Skills and Wealth & Esteem.

Patience: Partly because of this you should be serene and realistic. You should also recognize that your Employment Plot will usually cover a working lifetime. There is a natural tendency for employees to "gravitate" upwards in their Organisation due to the desire, outlined above, to promote internally. Patience is a virtue that will be valued by your company and responding to the frustration of what you regard as slow advancement can be counter-productive, especially if by changing Organisation/Occupation Track.

Reminder: Passing your ZSP. In Chapter 10 I argued against the Peter Principle and suggested that it was perfectly possible to progress past your ZSP. The key attribute in doing so was to be better (possess higher Skills) than your competitors.

Because you will have a higher perception of your Status than that of your boss and colleagues, it may be difficult for you to recognize when your ZSP has been reached. A common juncture is when you advance from managing things or processes to managing people. This requires a major change in Skills and it is strange that organisations do not do enough to prepare their staff for this steep jump.

As you move past your ZSP you enter the glorious realms of a **multiplier** in rewards: small increases in Skills drive a disproportionate increase in Wealth & Esteem. We often think that Captains of Industry are massively overpaid but you take a different view when you are one of them.

# 11.6  Changing Careers

Many of the choices to be made in deciding whether to change career can be drafted onto the same Plots as those for choosing your career.

You will usually change your Career often during your lifetime, increasingly so in an age where old industries die out and new ones emerge with new technologies. When this happens (or more importantly, when you consider such a change) you will need to create a new Employment Plot or draft the old and new Occupation Tracks on the same Plot. However, you will only need to do this if your change in Career is a definitive one, rather than a change in emphasis within the same Occupation Track.

There are several types of Career change, and I will consider four: Disruptive, Dismissal, Redundancy, Seismic Negative and Seismic Positive. To begin:

Disruptive Career Change This type of Career change happens when one simply chooses to move from one Occupation to another:

Case Study  The Good Life

Cedric and Cecilia are clearly successful. They live in a very big house in the nice suburbs, drive fancy cars and their two regulation children go to an expensive fee-paying boarding school. I know that Cecelia works in PR but I am less sure about Cedric. Something big in the City, I think, but when I ask him he does not make any sense. Be that as it may, they have made it.

On a holiday in foreign climes they visit a local farmers' market and are enthralled: all those home-grown goodies so attractively presented by such nice natives. That evening, a little bit over the mark on the prandials, they begin to fantasise about leaving the rat-race and running a small farm back home where, they imagine, there would be a high demand in their country for farm products grown to their impeccable taste.

After the hols they go as far as to make enquiries; to their surprise (but not mine) they discover that there are lots of small farms for sale (should have been a clue) and, by egging each other on, they quit their jobs and purchase the object of their desire, choosing mainly based on the charm of the ancient farmhouse.

As you might expect, things do not go well. The sheep run amok because the sheepdog bought from a wily neighbour was deaf, the cows do not fancy the bull one little bit (halitosis), the local fox invites all his mates over for a party in the poorly built chicken coup and the pigs behave like pigs in ... scoffing all the expensive wrong comestibles that Cedric and Cecelia thought were necessary for them. They grow all their vegetables in season only to find that their harvesting coincides with a glut. Finances are a nightmare and the children, when our couple remember them, have to leave their fancy college and go to the local school which, with very good reason, they are not enamoured of.

Worst of all they discover that their local farmers' market is heavily over-subscribed by other fools who have made the same mistake, and that it is viciously competitive. On the plus side they do manage to sell the farm to a couple just like themselves (the ancient farmhouse swayed it yet again) but on the downside, much to their surprise, their erstwhile companies have moved on and decline to re-employ them. Since then I have lost touch.

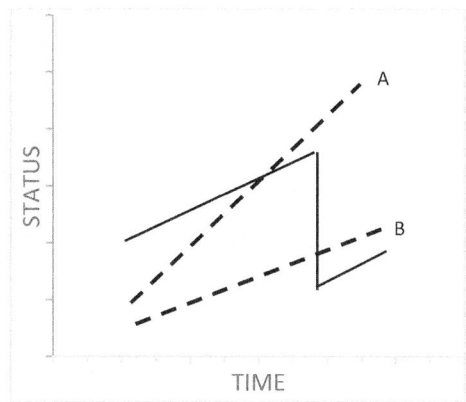

Employment Plot for Cedric (or Cecelia)

Commentary  In their Employment Plot we can see that Cedric (or Cecelia, let us just refer to him as he was the instigator as well as the cheerleader of the whole enterprise) has risen to just past his ZSP in his Occupation marked by the Track A. It is possible that he was self-aware enough to realise that he was unlikely to go any further.

Be that as it may, his Skills there were recognized and suitably rewarded. By moving to the farm (Occupation Track B) his **applicable** Skills plummeted and, even though that Occupation Track B required different Skills and provided lower Wealth & Esteem, he was not able to match those requirements.

If you do decide to consider changing your occupation a simple Employment Plot might throw a bucket of water over your plans. Be realistic about your Skills; that is all that matters in such circumstances.

Dismissal

Case Study: The Respectable Bank

Harry works as a clerk in the Respectable Bank and has ambitions to be promoted to Senior Clerk. It comes as a bit of a shock, therefore, when Helen is appointed from outside of the bank and she becomes his boss. Helen is very popular amongst Harry's peers. She is always the first to buy a round in the pub after work and gives expensive Christmas presents to all her staff in the season. She is well known for her generosity.

Perhaps too well known. Harry begins to sulk and becomes idle. So much so that on the last day of January (the HR department always sack staff on the last day of the month but not at Christmas time) Harry is dismissed for being work shy. Much to everyone's surprise Helen is dismissed on the same day. It turns out that she has been funding her generosity and other habits by fiddling accounts and siphoning off funds to her own credit.

Both Harry and Helen have to find another job but their sacking bodes ill in their efforts. Eventually Harry lands up as a Security Guard where his talents for doing nothing are better appreciated. Helen becomes much enamoured of life in gaol and becomes a prison warder.

Commentary   In Harry's case his dismissal is one of **omission** (not doing something expected) which exhibits a **lack of Skills**. In Helen's case her dismissal is due to the sin of **commission** (doing something not expected) which reflects badly on her **applicable** Skills. In both cases the perceived diminution of Skills results in lower Wealth & Esteem.

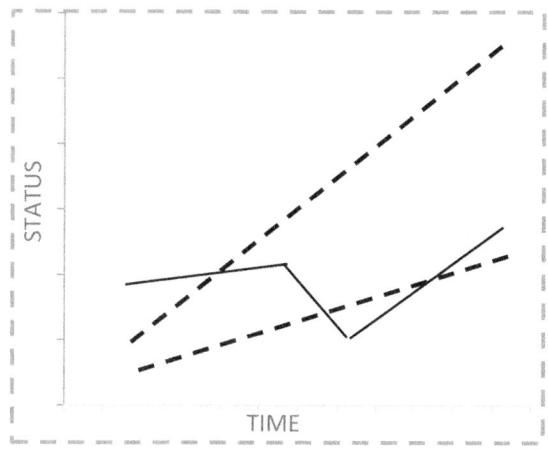

Career/Occupation Change for Harry or Helen

You may, from this Case Study, infer that it is better to be fired for sins of commission rather than of omission and you could be right. Best option, however, is not to get caught.

Redundancy

Another way for a Career/Occupation change to be forced upon you is to be made redundant. Again there are two types of redundancy to concern us: firstly is what I call **Macro** redundancy where your whole business goes up the spout. In contrast is what I call **Micro** redundancy where just your department (or, even worse, just you) are let go. In terms of Employment Plots the Occupation Track ceases and is replaced, we hope, by a new job. Since, with redundancy, it is the job and not the person that fails, there is no reduction in Skills and there should, therefore, be no reduction in Wealth & Esteem. It is worth saying though that, unhappily, a whiff of blame is sometimes assigned to those made redundant, especially of the Micro type.

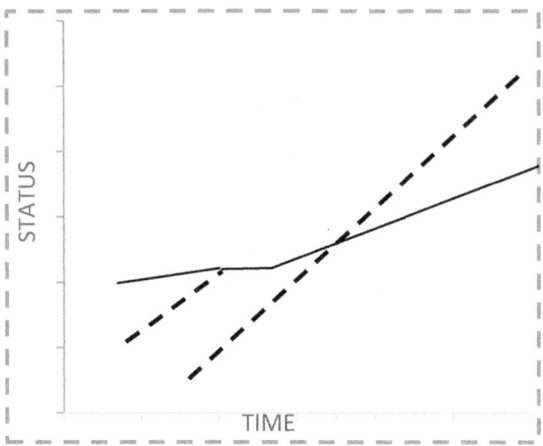

<u>Model Employment Plots of Person Made Redundant</u>

Career changes are deemed Seismic when the change is so radical that the original Occupation tack is abandoned and a completely new one is embarked upon. The key to recognising Seismic changes as opposed to normal ones is (a) that the first Occupation Track ceases (in normal Career changes the first Occupation Track continues even though the worker has left it) and (b) that the new Occupation Track is especially different to the old one.

Negative Seismic changes are ones where Skills and Wealth & Esteem reduce dramatically, and Positive ones are the happy occurrences where they markedly improve. The former are, unfortunately, much more common and we will begin with those.

<u>Case Study: Kansas Here We Come (Hopefully)</u>

Dorothy yearns to return to Kansas and to her Aunty Em and Uncle Henry. Her friend Scarecrow wants a brain, Tin Man desires a heart and Cowardly Lion longs for bravery. Toto the dog only wants a bone. The Good Witch of the North has told them where to find these essentials: the fabled Wizard of Oz, who resides in the Emerald City and has the power to grant their wishes. Off they set along the

Yellow Brick Road to reach the legendary capital and an appointment with the good sorcerer. A few inconveniences thrown in their path along the way by the Wicked Witch of the East (who is sulking because a tornado killed her sister) delay their progress and extend the story a bit but, at last, they come to the promised land.

The great Wizard of Oz prevaricates and negotiates his help in return for the broomstick of the surviving Wicked Witch but, at last, an audience is granted. Toto, in searching for a place to do his business (not having "been" on the Yellow Brick Road), accidently pulls down a curtain to reveal the old humbug (now an Oz of Wizard) to be a giant fraud whose levers and microphone are distinctly out of date. In vain he awards paper qualifications to Scarecrow and Cowardly Lion and a measly tin watch to Tin Man but is not much help to Dorothy. Bad Toto does not get a bone.

Please watch the film to find out how it all turns out in the end.

Commentary

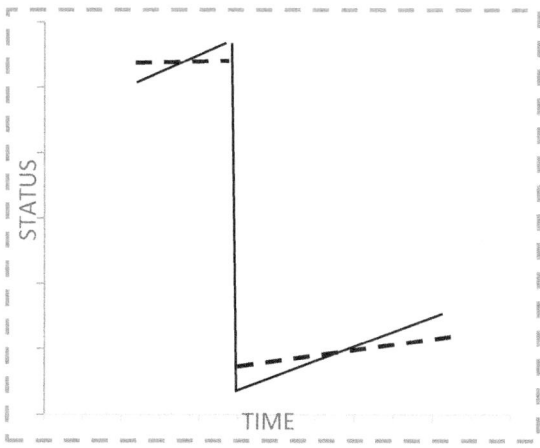

Employment Plots for the Wizard of Oz

This is a **Negative** seismic change. The Wizard's first Occupation comes to a shuddering halt due to Toto's bad lavatorial behaviour. His Skills are revealed fraudulent and drop precipitously with the consequent loss of Esteem (and also Wealth?). In a Seismic change he has to begin a new Occupation that matches his new perceived Skills.

Should a Seismic Negative change happen to you will have little alternative but to suck it up. Icarus flew too close to the sun. Beware of hubris.

## Case Study : Belle of the Ball

Once upon a time a young miss lived with her stepmother and two sisters in a large house. She had to do all the housework while her household relatives took considerable advantage. She did not have a lot going for her – even her name of Cinderella was not attractive. She would have preferred something sweet such as Susan or Amy but every time she went to the deed poll office to change it, which was not often due to the household chores, she never seemed to have the right paperwork. Bureaucracy, heh?

The only things going for her were her uncomplaining nature and, for the few enamoured of such personal features, small feet. Appearance-wise the grime and ashes did not help. Only the resident mice appreciated her.

The King of the realm had announced a massive rave headlined by Wolf and the Three Little Pigs. Tickets were like gold dust – Cinderella's family all got one but her spiteful stepmother told her she was too young to go and ignored her anguished sobs. "It's not **fair**!" she cried. "I'm **nearly** sixteen."

Off they went leaving Cinderella sulking by her fireplace. But then, Lo! A personal fairy godmother called by and jazzed her up a great deal with an haute-couture dress, the latest fashion in pink stretch limos and her own transport staff! Off she went to the rave with the catch (there's always one) that she had to return to her drudgery by midnight. What a ball she had! Which was the better: the envy of her relations or the attention from the Prince! Dance! It was just like John Travolta when everyone else forms a circle applauding the fantastic couple. However, the fairy godmother, in her haste with the transformations, had omitted the key accessory of a watch. Cinderella had to rush home as a convenient clock struck twelve times (surprisingly since it had not struck the preceding hours for her to keep tally) and she abandoned a slipper (fairy tale for a shoe) on the exit by the bouncers. Only a churl could suggest that she had had too much champagne.

Some perspicacious readers will have guessed by now where this is going. The Prince was smitten with the most glamourous apparition at the festivities. So much so that he scoured his father's kingdom to try to reconnect with her, social media not being what it is now. His only clue was the mislaid slipper, so finding a match became the sport du jour across the realm. Fortunately, it was a small realm, sort of Monaco size and similar royal family, so once tiny shod children had been eliminated (as the social mores required in the Kingdom forbade underage marriage) it did not take long to match up the glass slipper with Cinderella's tiny feet (I remind you one of the elements of her Esteem was daintiness in that department).

Rejoicing for Cinderella and her beau, big sulks from the family. Massive wedding, paparazzi everywhere, all colours of balloons, lots of cake and a honeymoon in Disneyland, where she is still remembered to this day. She obtained Life Wealth and Esteem from her new husband and, since she was not one to hold a grudge, allowed her family to obtain Vicarious Esteem mainly in the form of Wealth.

When her father-in-law died she became Queen and, despite the growing republican thing, she reigned and lived happily ever after (which in is an indeterminate timeframe in Fairyland).

Now for the truth: "lived happily ever after" is the convention which signals "we are stopping here because continuation would go into things and places that do not conform to the happy construction of the tale so far".

In fact, Cinderella turned out to be a poor queen, becoming very vain and pompous; her biggest fault was that she did not produce the expected son and heir. She froze out her stepsisters and dissed her stepmother. The populous tired of her showing off her tiny feet and became rebellious; the Prince divorced her. I won't go on . . . . . .

Commentary

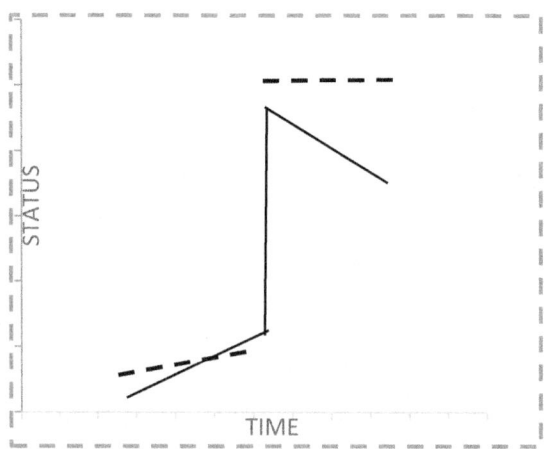

Employment Plot for Cinderella

This is a **Positive** seismic change. In her first Occupation Cinderella's low Skills are matched by her low Wealth & Esteem; this Occupation ends dramatically on the discovery of her petite tootsies, and there is a Seismic shift to Princess and then Queen. Unsurprisingly her Skills in her new Occupation do not match her new Wealth & Esteem and that mismatch worsens.

Seismic changes in Careers/Occupations are rare. Negative examples are, as with our Wizard, caused by unjustified reputations being rumbled. Positive changes usually involve success in lotteries and the like. You cannot win unless you are in the game.

## 11.7 Retirement

Case Study: Release

Bob is a teacher of French in his school and has risen to the position of Deputy Head. From the beginnings of a degree in his chosen language and a teaching diploma he has always been a teacher and has now, at the required age, had to retire from the school and his profession.

His progress up the ranks in education has been slow but steady. He had applied for headships at his and other schools on a few occasions but was always unsuccessful. His reputation was one of adequacy at the deputy level but without the necessaries for headship.

There are small celebrations and presentations to mark his retirement, but Bob is self-aware enough to know that, as he walks through the school gates for the last time, the earth and the school have moved on.

Commentary

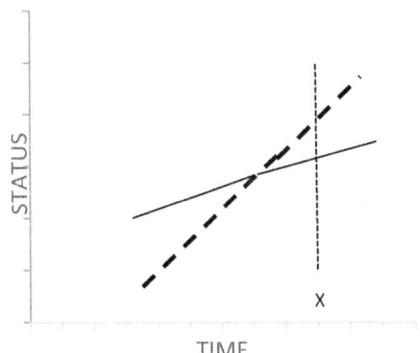

STATUS

TIME

Employment Plot for Bob, Retiring at X

Bob follows the usual progress in his Career along a single Occupation Track, passing his ZSP but then failing to advance further.

Retirement (at time X) involves significant alterations to his Work Status Profile: Work Wealth drops to zero, Work Esteem leaves but a shadow. All this follows the extinction of his **applicable** Work Skills.

Which leaves Bob relying on his Life Status which has probably been neglected whilst he was working. Hopefully he has transferred part of his Work Wealth (his salary) into Life Wealth through pensions. His route to reviving his Total Status lies in increasing his Life Skills and therefore Life Status.

If Bob follows the usual pattern he will look back on his career not with nostalgia but with incredulity that he spent so much effort in climbing the ladder. His Self Esteem as a teacher came from his talents in that role not from a position in a hierarchy. **Self Esteem trumps all.**

## 11.8  Conclusions and Chapter's Key Points

This chapter has described the usage of Employment Plots at several possible points in different careers. I maintain that the drafting of these Plots clarifies and focuses the elements involved in career decision analysis. Plots can be contrasted with other possible scenarios and, usefully, with those of your peers and competitors.

**Draft Employment Plots throughout your Career**

**Plan the Change from Work to Life Status Profiles**

## 11.9  Death

The general rule is that your Career Path/Occupation Plot ends when you die and, indeed, it does as far as you are concerned. But part of your reputation lives on:

Final Case Study:  Sainthood

The Lady known as Mother Teresa (1910 – 1997) founded an Order of Nuns who ran homes for people dying of diseases. The Roman Catholic nuns swore chastity, a life of poverty and obedience to aid the poorest of the poor.

Mother Teresa became world famous for her sacrifices and was awarded the 1979 Nobel Peace prize and, an honour that she would have rated higher had she lived, was canonized in 2016. (Thanks yet again, Wikipedia. All Hail!)

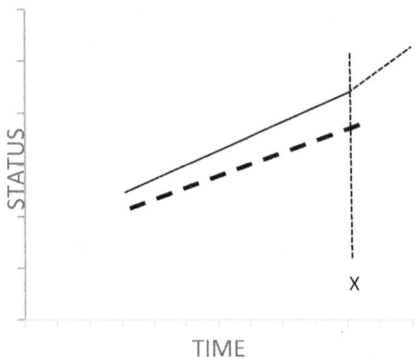

### Employment Plot for Mother Teresa

Mother Teresa dies at time point X; Skills and what little Wealth she had cease at that point, but her Esteem goes on.

Usually the strength and length of post mortem Esteem is proportional to its level at the time of death. I should warn you that if you try in your lifetime to establish your credentials for sainthood it is a very crowded field and success is not assured. Your family will, however, remember you with, I am sure, positive Esteem.

That seems a good time to stop.

Printed in Great Britain
by Amazon